THE CHIMES

Ringing to God's Glory

DAVID PAGENKOPF

BALBOA.
PRESS

A DIVISION OF HAY HOUSE

Balboa Press books may be ordered through booksellers or by contacting:

Balboa Press
A Division of Hay House
1663 Liberty Drive
Bloomington, IN 47403
www.balboapress.com
1 (877) 407-4847

Because of the dynamic nature of the Internet, any web addresses or links contained in this book may have changed since publication and may no longer be valid. The views expressed in this work are solely those of the author and do not necessarily reflect the views of the publisher, and the publisher hereby disclaims any responsibility for them.

Scripture quotations are taken from the Holy Bible, New Living Translation, copyright ©1996, 2004, 2007, 2013, 2015 by Tyndale House Foundation. Used by permission of Tyndale House Publishers, Inc., Carol Stream, Illinois 60188. All rights reserved.

The author of this book does not dispense medical advice or prescribe the use of any technique as a form of treatment for physical, emotional, or medical problems without the advice of a physician, either directly or indirectly. The intent of the author is only to offer information of a general nature to help you in your quest for emotional and spiritual well-being. In the event you use any of the information in this book for yourself, which is your constitutional right, the author and the publisher assume no responsibility for your actions.

Any people depicted in stock imagery provided by Thinkstock are models, and such images are being used for illustrative purposes only.
Certain stock imagery © Thinkstock.

Print information available on the last page.

ISBN: 978-1-5043-9529-8 (sc)
ISBN: 978-1-5043-9531-1 (hc)
ISBN: 978-1-5043-9530-4 (e)

Library of Congress Control Number: 2018900983

Balboa Press rev. date: 07/28/2018

I n the last chapter of Mark's Gospel, we read of Jesus' ascension into heaven. Gathered with him atop the mountain are his disciples; and it is at this time that Jesus makes known to them his Great Commission, wherein they are told to go into the world and make disciples of all nations. My Study Bible explains it this way: This is not an option, but a command to all who call Jesus "Lord." That includes you and me, doesn't it? While we may not be evangelists in the true sense of the word, we have all received gifts we can use to help fulfill this great commission that Jesus has given us.

For the last seventeen years or so, I have had the privilege of writing a column for our church's monthly newsletter, called *the Chimes*. In each of them I have tried to focus my thoughts on the concept of evangelism. "Why", you might ask, would I want to do something like this?

Let me try to explain it this way: I believe God has gifted us all in many ways; and I believe he expects us to use these gifts in a way that will glorify him and fulfill the purpose he has in mind for us. To some he has given the gift of kindness; to others the gift of preaching, or perhaps teaching; or care giving, healing or service. One could go on and on.

Some have said that I have a gift of writing. We'll see. All I know is it has always been easier for me to express myself in writing than it has been to do it orally.

What follows is a list of some several dozen of these articles. In each of them I have tried to focus on what I believe to be an urgent need to tell others about Jesus Christ and what he has done for us through his life, his teachings, his suffering, his death on the cross, and, through his resurrection and his victory over death for all believers. The apostle, John, says it so beautifully in the third chapter of his Gospel (v. 16).

It made sense to me to separate these articles into groups, as opposed to chapters found in the table of contents of most books.

Some, you will notice, may be of interest to just about *everyone*; others relate more closely to *family*, or perhaps to our *church* family. Still others focus on the greatest historical event of all time, Easter. And finally, a few of my thoughts on the most beautiful of all things. - *Love.*

CONTENTS

FAMILY

CHURCH

LOVE

ACKNOWLEDGEMENTS

O ne thing I have learned as a fledgling writer is that it can't be done alone. Even before one gets into the intricacies of editing, marketing, cover design, publishing, and distribution, there is much more a novice needs – things like encouragement, inspiration, opportunity, constructive criticism, and much more.

Even if my writing is never published, it won't be for lack of encouragement, especially from, my lovely wife Laura of more than 60 years, who has encouraged me to do what she knew I wanted to do. I also felt a reassurance from our three children, Linda, John, and Andy.

It was John who would say, "Keep 'em coming." whenever he received a completed article.

Encouragement, indeed!

More encouragement and lots of help. Thank you Andy and Laura, I couldn't have done it without you.

And it was Andy who first mentioned publication. More encouragement!

Linda often passed on to me reaching-out stories of her family and church, several of which I have included in the finished manuscript.

My columns would never have been written had it not been for the energy and passion for outreach felt by our two pastors at St. Paul's – the Rev. Dr. David Jost and Rev. David Stoner. What a privilege to hear them lead worship on Sunday morning and Bible studies during the week. I am so grateful to Pastor Jost for allowing me to write for our monthly newsletter, the *CHIMES*. Encouragement, in and of itself!

And so many thanks to our church secretary, Corrine Mattson, for her patience and acceptance of my articles, even when they were late or too long.

My dear friend, Eva Priestley, richly deserves my heartfelt thanks for her skillful editing of my manuscript.

My sincere gratitude to former pastors Roy Christensen and David Mangiante, and also to many members and former members for their uplifting comments over the years.

And to all my church family which I've called friend throughout the years, you've made this journey very special.

Thank you.

INTRODUCTION

I t all began many years ago during a Wednesday morning Bible Study with Pastor David Stoner. For the life of me, I can't recall the context in which he said it; but, what he said has stuck with me ever since. He simply said, "The reason we are here on earth is to glorify God." Now I may have been told this before; but it never registered with me the way it did that Wednesday morning. To be honest, I couldn't remember ever feeling a need to glorify God; but as I think back, I probably heard similar admonitions such as "being reborn" or "transformed" in some way. Bottom line! From that day forward, I began to feel a real urgency that it was time to begin putting Christ first in my life.

About that same time, I was asked by one of my church friends if I would consider joining his evangelism team. Realizing that this might be part of God's plan for me, I accepted his invitation. Soon afterward, my lovely wife, Laura, asked if she could help out; and we both became quite active, she perhaps more than I.

To keep our members informed of our outreach activities, the team decided to introduce an article into the church's monthly newsletter, the *Chimes*. Having once been awarded an "A" for writing a one act play in high school, I was assigned the task.

As the months passed, I became more comfortable with writing. Several of our friends at church were very kind with their remarks, and I even heard from some former members who were on the church's mailing list. As much as I appreciated their kindness, I had to confess to them that it was really the Holy Spirit's work, not mine.

If you will turn in your Bible to the last chapter of Matthew, he records two extraordinary events that took place soon after Christ's death on the cross: the first, of course, being his resurrection from the tomb in which he was buried just three days earlier – arguably, the greatest historical event of all time. "Don't be afraid," the angel said to Mary Magdalene and the other Mary having come to visit the tomb. "He isn't here." He is risen from the dead, just as he said would happen." (Matthew 28: 5-6)

The second event may not seem quite as sensational; but, in my mind, at least, is of momentous importance. I am referring to the Great Commission which Jesus gave to his twelve apostles. (By this time, Mathias had been chosen to replace the deceased Judas Iscariot, who had betrayed Jesus). And the twelve were no longer referred to as disciples, meaning follower or learner, but were now full-fledged apostles; that is, messenger, or missionary." Jesus tells all twelve he wants them to go and make disciples of all nations…. baptizing them in the name of the Father, and the Son, and the Holy Spirit. Jesus adds, "Teach these new disciples to obey all the commands I have given you."

Now that's quite an order, isn't it? But, then Jesus states. "And be sure of this: "I am with you always, even to the end of the age." (v. 20) Of course, this is precisely what these men did as they reached out to people around the world as it was known then. They told the Good News story of Jesus, his birth, his life, his teachings, his miracles, his suffering and death, and, with his resurrection, his victory over death for all believers. They brought people to Christ. They started churches and nurtured them, fully committing their lives to the Lord and growing his kingdom.

For more than two thousand years, Jesus' disciples have been "bearing fruit" for him. They have been making disciples who, in turn, have been making more disciples. Let us not forget we *are* Christ's church; and I believe he wants us, you and me, to continue to grow his church.

And that brings me to the purpose of this book.

When the lord says to me "go...." as he did to his original twelve, I believe he is asking me to become a "fisher of men" just as he said to Peter and Andrew as they were mending their nets on the shore of Galilee. They were just ordinary guys like me and you; but Jesus had plans for them. For the next three years he would have them to himself, equipping them to fulfill his purpose – the making of disciples. It is my hope and prayer that, through the writing of this book, I might fulfill his purpose for me. And, I thank Him for giving me the time to do it.

I'm getting a late start, so let's get going.

EVERYONE

CHRIST AT HEART'S DOOR

" Listen! I am standing at the door and knocking. If you hear my voice and open the door, I will come in to you and eat with you and you with me." It is this verse from Revelations 20:3 that inspired the memorable painting of Warner Salman, Christ at Heart's Door.

The loving-kindness of Jesus knocking on the door of anyone's heart, seeking admittance, is almost too much to take in. Why would he do this? What is there about any of us that would appeal to Jesus? Aren't we among those who sent him to the cross? The answer, of course: He loves us.

William L. Hogan said in one of his sermons that Jesus is interested in us and wants to be our friend. He draws his listeners' attention to the painting and notes an intensely and insightful detail: no latch can be seen on the door. The artist is telling us that the door must be opened from within. Christ will not force himself upon us; but neither will he cease striving to gain entrance into our heart.

Scripture tells us that we should try to be more like Christ and that we should not be ashamed of witnessing to others of what

Christ has done for us. Doesn't this say that he would like us to finish what he and his disciples began years ago and continue knocking at the doors of unbelievers to light the way for them to find their Savior?

COMPOUND INTEREST

O ne of the most important lessons we can teach our children and grandchildren, I believe, is the concept of compound interest – that is, the manner in which money saved or invested wisely may compound in value many times over if left untouched.

As youngsters, most of us learned from our parents the wisdom of opening a savings account in a local bank, but I, for one, never fully understood until later in life how my savings would grow in interest earned over time. There was always something I needed right now like maybe new roller skates or a brand new Louisville Slugger baseball bat.

Jesus touches on this with his Parable of the Talents in the twenty-fifth chapter of Matthew.

Before leaving on a journey a property owner entrusted to three of his slaves a varied amount of talents to attend to during his absence. Two of the slaves exercised good judgment with the talents in their custody and were able to return to their master more than what had been given them. The master was so pleased that he committed even more things to their care in the future. But the third slave could only return the single talent he was given, and his master was very displeased.

Warren Buffett, investor and philanthropist, gives us a modern day example of how money, when managed wisely, can produce enormous results. As an eleven-year-old boy, Buffett made his first investment in the stock market. Some twenty-five years later, he owned his own company and, over time, he parlayed a $100 investment into a $40 billion net worth. And he did this while living a modest lifestyle.

What really made this man such a legend is his field, however, was evidenced when it became known that he contributed the bulk of his roughly $40 billion fortune to philanthropy, committing more than $30 billion to the Bill and Melinda Gates Foundation, thereby doubling the foundation's mission to improve global health.

I have gone into some detail here to try to illustrate how money, when managed prudently, can do some marvelous things. Now let's see how we might apply this principle of compound interest to the realm of evangelism.

Jesus tells us in John 15, "I am the vine, you are the branches. Those who abide in me and I in them bear much fruit...." In his Concise Commentary on the Whole Bible, Matthew Henry says that, as branches of this vine, we are to be fruitful by honoring God and doing good. How would you define being "fruitful?" Doesn't it mean producing more buds – more fruit – more disciples for Christ?

And let's not forget this principle of compound interest. If we can bring forth more believers, doesn't it stand to reason that some of them are going to do likewise? Sure it does. By compounding, over time even more disciples will be brought to Christ.

But, you know what!? In order for trees and vines to grow and buds to blossom and flourish, they need nourishment, don't they? They need water. Is Christ's church any different? I don't think so. The church also needs nourishment, and this nourishment issues from prayer. Jesus continues in John 15:7: "If you abide in me, and my words abide in you, ask for whatever you wish, and it will be done for you." How's that for good news?

WHAT ON EARTH ARE WE HERE FOR?

S ome months are more difficult than others for me to find something fresh and interesting to write about. As I lay in bed one morning last week, nothing suggested itself to me; so I got up, went into the den and picked up one of the books I had been reading -- The Purpose-Driven Life by Rick Warren, the founding pastor of Saddleback Church in Lake Forest, California.

Pastor Warren's book takes us on a journey to find the answer to life's most important question: What on earth are we here for? He tells us at the outset that God had a purpose for each one of us while we were still in our mother's womb. As you might guess, His plan is to use each of us to tell others about the Good News of Jesus Christ. And we are to use the gifts and talents that God has given us to accomplish His purpose for us.

Nothing new really! We've heard this many times over the years from Pastor Jost, Pastor Stoner and Pastor Mangiante and all of their predecessors here at St. Paul's. For that matter, everything written in Pastor Warren's book we have already heard from Jesus - or from Paul or other writers of scripture.

But please! Take my word for it. You will never regret having read this book. Some have said that it is destined to be a classic on the Christian life -- It is life-changing -- a masterpiece of wise counsel. My thought on it: Pastor Warren's light shines on every page.

All through school it was my habit to underline key points in the texts assigned to us. Every page of my book written by Pastor Warren is a mess with red underlines, brackets and notes written in the margin. It's that good.

But it was in the 36th chapter last week that I found what I thought might interest you. Let me whet your appetite a little with a few of Pastor Warren's insights. He tells us:

* we were made for a mission: to finish what Jesus started. John 17:18; Acts 20:24. (Pastor Warren relates almost all of his remarks directly to the Bible).
* Our mission is to serve unbelievers; our ministry is to serve believers.
* Just as the twelve-year old Jesus told his parents while in the temple that he had to be about his Father's business, so must we do the same. And just as Jesus proclaimed from the cross twenty-one years later that "It is finished", so must we try our utmost to be able to say this when our purpose in life has been accomplished.

Jesus' Great Commission (Mt.28:19-20) to "go and make disciples ... teaching them to obey everything I have commanded you" is not optional for us. It's a command and, if we ignore it, we are being disobedient to God. I mean, when I think about this, I get in trouble if I disobey my wife! How much worse if I disobey God?!

The greatest thing that we can do for others who need Jesus is to tell them how eternal life can be theirs. Pastor Warren makes this analogy: If we know someone who is dying from cancer and we know the cure, it would be a crime to withhold that information. How much worse to deny our friends the Good News that is ours to share.

One thought that came to mind as I read this book: We have all had a job - an occupation - during our lives, whether as a teacher, a mechanic, a secretary, a homemaker - whatever. Pastor Warren is telling us that we also have a second job -- to share the Good News of Jesus Christ whenever we can.

Jesus would like us to do this, too, don't you think?

CHOICES AND CONSEQUENCES

Our Lord tells us in his second commandment that we are not to use his name in vain. Why is it then that we so often hear this commandment violated? I'll grant you there are some who may not have received this instruction early in life. But what about those of us who know better? They make a bad choice when they blaspheme God. And I believe for every bad choice, there is a consequence.

Choices and consequences! They both play an important role in our lives, don't they? When we choose to disobey the law, we do so at the risk of inviting serious consequences. When a parent repeatedly overlooks bad behavior in a child, inevitably there will be bad consequences down the road.

I believe also that a bad choice is made when someone elects not to come to church. Will there be consequences for this? Who knows? After all, our God is a loving God – a forgiving God. Certainly, it's not for us to judge others. I could be wrong about this, but I believe a decision to habitually miss worship services distances that person from God.

God wants us to sanctify the Holy Day. (third commandment). Why can't we all find one hour on a week-end to hear God's word and sing his praises, to experience his forgiveness at the Communion rail, and enjoy the fellowship of other believers?

I recently read an article which I believe is right on target. The writer suggests that we try to imagine: If everyone were to receive a personal invitation to meet with the president at the White House, that would be really exciting. Many people (not everyone, perhaps) would count it a great privilege to meet their head of state. And yet, when the King of kings, the Lord of lords, the Creator of the universe, extends a special invitation to come to his House of worship, many decline the invitation.

When we hear or learn of such a person, let's pray, in Jesus' name, that that person will open his heart and invite God to dwell in him. We know God loves him. And we know he answers prayers, but it will be in His time. How do we know this? Because our prayer is in keeping with His will.

A MAN WHO CAME HOME

C an a book review be evangelical? Why not?

The Comeback is the story of Jay Robinson who, at the age of twenty-three, found fame and fortune in Hollywood for his role as Caligula, the mad, anti-Christian emperor in 20th Century Fox's movie spectacular, The Robe. But it's also the story of a man who feared and resented God, believing that by determination, shrewdness, and deceit, he could find happiness and success on his own.

The movie opened to ecstatic reviews. Hollywood gossip columnist, Luella Parsons, wrote of Robinson, "A star is born." Hedda Hopper agreed, describing Robinson in her column as "the most polished young actor of our times."

Sadly, Robinson soon became consumed by the role he played and by the money and adulation it brought him. Like Caligula, Robinson felt invincible. He fancied his expensive Bel Air estate as his own imperial palace.

His world would soon come tumbling down, however, as he plunged into the depths of drug addiction, eventually leading to his arrest for narcotics possession, and a prison sentence. Caligula's money was gone, and so was his palace.

Enter the real star of this story – Pauline Flowers, a young lady who worked as a nurse for the physician who was treating Jay for the damage done to his body by the drugs he had consumed. Pauline was also a Christian. A romance ensued, and soon they were married.

Pauline saw her husband as a man who needed Christ in his life, and she prayed for him constantly. It was about the time when Jay once again returned to prison that Pauline, herself, was stricken with tuberculosis, and Jay began to see for himself what he had become, - a failure, a drug addict, a man unable to care for himself and his young son.

Upon his release from prison, job opportunities, albeit menial, began to materialize for Jay. Pauline's prayers were being answered. Through a series of fortuitous meetings, Jay was cast in Born Again, in the role of David Shapiro, attorney and close friend of Charles Colson, President Nixon's "hatchet man" in the Watergate scandal. Colson, himself, had turned to Christ while serving a prison sentence, and he subsequently described Robinson's story as "the story of a man who has not only come back, but has come home."

And, sure enough, the role of Colson was played by Dean Jones, yet another Christian who urged Jay to embrace Christ. This eventually led to Jay Robinson's final acceptance of Christ in the office of Bob Munger, Executive Producer of Born Again, and also a Christian.

All of these men played important roles in bringing Jay Robinson "home." I believe, however, the unceasing prayers of his devoted wife, Pauline, were the ones that finally saved him.

THIS IS MOST CERTAINLY TRUE

"He is not here; for He has been raised.... Go quickly and tell His disciples.... (Matthew 28:5) Once again we have heard the joyful news proclaimed by the angel to the women at Jesus' tomb. How privileged we are to be able to hear this story every Spring and to be able to shout as one "He is risen! He is risen, indeed!"

In his first letter to the Christians in Asia Minor Peter calls to mind this Easter story: "He himself bore our sins in His body on the cross.... by His wounds we have been healed." (v.24)

My purpose in citing this story of Peter's is this: I believe he is trying to help me (and you, too, I hope) respond to his challenge in chapter three of this same letter: "And if someone asks about your Christian hope, always be ready to explain it. But do this in a gentle and respectful way." (v v.15-16) And here is our response, right here in Matthew's account of Jesus' victory over death for each one of us. And with it, as believers, we have hope, don't we?

The hope being the promise of eternal life with Him in heaven. Clearly, that should be our response – because we know it to be true. Peter was there. It is God's inspired word written for us by Peter who witnessed the whole thing. Isn't that the hope we can declare to anyone who asks?

That should be enough to convince anyone. But I would like to suggest that there is more that we might add to our response. How about our belief in our Triune God as we express it in our Apostle's Creed?

The First Article: I believe in God the Father Almighty, maker of heaven and earth. In his Small Catechism Dr. Martin Luther then asks: What does this mean? And he goes on to explain: I believe that God has made me and all creatures; that He has given me my body and soul, eyes, ears, and all my members, my reason and all my senses, and still takes care of them. He also gives me clothing and shoes, food and drink, house and home, wife and children, land, animals, and all I have. He richly endows me with all that I need ..... He defends me against all danger and guards and protects me from all evil. All this He does out of fatherly, divine goodness and mercy, without any merit or worthiness in me. For all this it is my duty to thank and praise Him. This is most certainly true.

There you have it. Everything that we need and have is given to us by God our Father. The Second Article relates to our Lord Jesus, also a gift from our Father (John 3:16): And in Jesus Christ, His only Son, our Lord, Who was conceived by the Holy Spirit, born of the Virgin Mary, suffered under Pontius Pilate, was crucified, died and was buried. He descended into hell. The third day He rose again from the dead. He ascended into heaven and sits at the right hand of God the Father Almighty. From thence He shall come to judge the living and the dead.

And Dr. Luther explains for us the meaning of this Second Article: I believe that Jesus Christ, true God, begotten of the

Father from eternity, and also true man, born of the Virgin Mary, is my Lord, who has redeemed me, a lost and condemned creature, purchased and won me from all sins, from death, and from the power of the devil; not with gold or silver, but with His holy, precious blood and with His innocent suffering and death, that I may be His own and live under Him in His kingdom and serve Him in everlasting righteousness, innocence, and blessedness, just as He has risen from the dead, lives and reigns to all eternity. This is most certainly true.

And finally, the Third Article of the Creed: I believe in the Holy Spirit, the holy catholic church, the communion of saints, the forgiveness of sins, the resurrection of the dead, and the life everlasting.

And Dr. Luther's explanation of this Third Article: I believe that by my own understanding or strength I cannot believe in my Lord Jesus Christ or come to Him, but instead the Holy Spirit has called me through the gospel, enlightened me with His gifts, made me holy and kept me in the true faith, just as He calls, gathers, enlightens, and makes holy the whole Christian church on earth and keeps it with Jesus Christ in the one common, true faith. Daily in this Christian church the Holy Spirit abundantly forgives all sins – mine and those of all believers. On the last day the Holy Spirit will raise me and all the dead and will give to me and all believers in Christ eternal life. This is most certainly true.

So, right here, in these three Articles of the Creed, we have our answer to anyone who questions our hope. As a boy participating in Confirmation classes, Pastor Romoser made us memorize these Articles and their meaning; so he must have felt they were very important. Please don't ask me to recite them from memory now but, what's the matter with giving your copy of Luther's Small Catechism to anyone who questions our hope. You can get another copy from the church office.

OUTREACH DEFINED

In a Christian context there are various statements that may appropriately define the term Outreach.

* proclaiming the Good News of Jesus Christ.... Matthew 16:15-16
* reaching the unchurched – the unbelievers;
* witnessing to Christ and what He has done for all believers;
* telling your faith story – what Christ has done for you;
* acknowledging Jesus to others - Matthew 10:32;
* being about our Father's business – Luke 2:41-49;
* finishing God's mission – the work that Jesus began;
* being what we say we are – evangelical;
* inviting -- welcoming;
* loving your neighbor.

But, before any of this happens, we must pray that God's will be done through us; and we must be alert for opportunities he will give us to reach out -- and then we must listen! We must understand that outreach begins with someone else – and we must listen to that someone else before we respond. God will equip us with the right response. He will tell us when to invite – when to say "Come and see."

EXCUSE ME! ARE YOU JESUS?

A nd so begins the story that follows. It's a story of kindness.
A few years ago, a group of salesmen went to a regional sales convention in Chicago. They had assured their wives they would be home in plenty of time for Friday night's dinner. In their rush, with tickets and briefcases, one of these salesmen inadvertently kicked over a table which held a display of apples. Apples flew everywhere. Without stopping or looking back, they all managed to reach the plane in time for their nearly-missed boarding. All but one! He paused, took a deep breath, and experienced a deep compassion for the girl whose apple stand had been overturned.

He told his buddies to go on without him, waved good-bye, told one of them to call his wife when they arrived at their home destination, and explain his taking a later flight. Then he returned to the terminal where the apples were all over the terminal floor.

He was glad he did.

The sixteen--year-old girl was totally blind! She was softly crying, tears running down her cheeks in frustration, and at the same time helplessly groping for her spilled produce as the crowd swirled about her, no one stopping, and no one caring for her plight.

The salesman knelt on the floor with her, gathered up the apples, put them back on the table, and helped organize her display. As he did this, he noticed that many of them had become battered and bruised. These he set aside in another basket.

When he had finished, he took out his wallet and said to the girl, 'Here, please take this $40 for the damage we did. Are you ok?' She nodded through her tears. He continued on with, "I hope we didn't spoil your day too badly."

As the salesman started to walk away, the bewildered girl called out to him, 'Mister ......" He paused and turned to look into those blind eyes. She continued, 'Are you Jesus?'

He stopped in mid stride, and he wondered. Then, slowly, he made his way to catch the later flight with that question burning and bouncing about his soul, "Are you Jesus?" That's our destiny, is it not? To be so like Jesus that others cannot tell the difference as we live and interact with the world that is blind to his love, life, and grace.

ONE - STOP SHOPPING

When you think about it, just about everything we need in life can be found at our local Shop Rite or Acme. One - stop shopping! Pretty amazing! Oh, once in a while we may have to run over to CVS to fill a prescription – or to Lowe's for a bag of lawn fertilizer – things like that. But almost everything else we can find at the supermarket. And if you're a coupon cutter like my wife, you can find some pretty good bargains – Buy one, get one free, 50% off on this item or that. Added savings, if you have a store card.

It occurred to me a few weeks ago that food shopping is not too unlike our study of God's Word.

One - stop shopping in our Bible will satisfy all, or at least most of our spiritual needs as a Christian. And we can find some really good values here, too. And what's really neat is that a lot of what we find in the Bible is free Think about it!

Take forgiveness, for example – already paid for in full by Jesus on the cross. And God's grace – free to all believers, even though we don't deserve it. And even God's love is free. All he asks is that we love him back, and others, too, just as he commands. But this shouldn't be too hard given everything he has done for us. And what about the gift of the Holy Spirit, given free to Christ's disciples on Pentecost and to all of us when we were baptized? And of course, Jesus himself! God, his Father, gave him, his only son, to us (John 3:16) and with the son, he gave us the promise of eternal life in heaven for all believers. And it's all free!!! Talk about a bargain!

And we are told there are a lot of people who are not aware of all these treasures. And there are many others anxious to find out more. But they may not even have a Bible – or a church. These are people Jesus wants us to love. And if we do that, why wouldn't we do everything in our power to share with them this Good News that is ours? Time may be running short.

COURAGE

William Bennett has quite a resume including positions as Secretary of Education under President Reagan and also co-director of Empower America. He has also written a book - - The Book of Virtues - - an inspiring anthology that treats of ten virtues: self- discipline; compassion; responsibility; friendship; work; courage; perseverance; honesty; loyalty; and faith. He says the book is intended for the moral education of our youth; but I didn't read it until I was retired and found it to be a really good read.

Courage is one virtue in particular that captured my interest because I feel it is so needful to any of us who have opportunity to speak to others about Jesus. So I asked Pastor Jost and his Monday Night Bible Study group what they thought about this: As Christians, must we have courage to witness effectively for Christ?

As you might expect, the consensus was "yes." At one point pastor stated that he believed that courage is a quality one needs to do something that needs doing even though it runs counter to what seems normal in our society. His view closely parallels the thinking of one of Mr. Bennett's contributors, one Phoebe Cary, who described courage this way: seeing what is right and doing it with firm resolve, despite the opinions of others.

So, you can take your pick, or define it yourself. I kind of like movie star John Wayne's take on the subject. He says courage is being scared to death, but saddling up anyway.

Jesus tells his listeners in Mark 8:35 that "those who want to save their life will lose it, and those who lose their life for my sake, and for the sake of the gospel, will save it." A text that would make for an interesting small group discussion, don't you think?

Let me close with a statement of Mr. Bennett's in his Introduction to his chapter on courage. He says "The mere inclination to do the right thing is not in itself enough. We have to know what the right thing to do is. We need wisdom - - often the wisdom of a wise leader - - to give our courage determinate form, to give it intelligent direction."

As Christians, we have such a wise leader, don't we? Jesus Christ, who went to the cross for us because he knew that it was his Father's will - - and the right thing to do.

Courage!!

SHARING YOUR FAITH IN DAILY LIFE

Being a part of St. Paul's Evangelism team has been one of the most spiritually uplifting experiences of my life. I honestly believe that it has helped me grow in faith and, more than anything else, it has impressed indelibly in my mind the need for me to be more alert to the opportunities God gives me to witness my faith. Oh, don't get me wrong! I'm still a long way from being the kind of disciple I want to be or that God wants me to be. But I'm learning, thanks to pastor and Kathy and others on our team. And, what's more important, I'm finding that I want to learn more about what it takes to speak about God to others.

That's why I was anxious to be part of the study group last January when Pastor Jost offered a course on Sharing Faith in Daily Life. This sounded like something that would help me become a better witness – something that I knew for certain was one of my weaknesses. And it helped me in so many ways. Let me tell you a little of what I have learned.

* If we are reluctant to speak of God's truth to others (and many of us Lutherans are), we need to begin with prayer. We need to ask God to give us the words to say and the courage to say them.
* We need to realize that there are a lot of people out there who are open to hearing the word of God. And who's going to tell them if we don't?
* And God uses ordinary people like us to talk to them. Moses was such a person. Exodus 3 tells us that he was reluctant to obey God's command to lead the Israelites out

21

of Egypt. He complained to God that he was not up to the task …. he was not eloquent." But God assures Moses that He will give him the words….He will teach him.

* And in the 10th chapter of Matthew Jesus tells his disciples "do not worry about how you are to speak or what you are to say…. For it is not you who speaks but the Spirit of the Father speaking through you." Now I had never given much thought to the fact that God can help us in this way. Maybe you had; but I hadn't.

* And how about this! God places us in relationships where we can witness for Him – just as he did with Philip and the Ethiopian eunuch in Acts 8:26. But we have to be ready. To make ourselves ready, we should give some serious thought to our own faith story and how it is that we came to place God first in our lives – and what it is that really makes us Christian… 1 Peter 3:15-16 says "we should be ready to make our defense to anyone who demands an accounting for the hope that is in you." It seems to me that we need to rehearse. We need to practice our own faith story to lock it in our minds so that we'll be all cocked and ready to go when opportunity knocks.

When I get going on something like this, I'm always afraid of sounding too pious. And I really don't mean to be. All of those Bible verses quoted above were given to those of us in the study group. They are not something that I researched on my own.

What a pleasure it has been these past few weeks to be able to listen to the words of faith spoken by our fellow parishioners during the Lenten worship services. Pastor Jost is really helping us with our evangelism ministry by providing this safe place for sharing our faith within our own congregation. Could it be that God is working through him to help us tell His story to others?

PETER'S COUNSEL

We are often told we witness our faith to others by the way we live our lives – by our thoughts, our words, and our actions. I think we would all agree we learn how to do this when we go to church and hear God's word spoken, and when we study his word in Scripture. In short, when we try to live Christ-like lives.

But the devil often has different plans for us, doesn't he? And our faith is sometimes challenged. In his first letter, Peter counsels, "... if someone asks about your Christian hope, always be ready to explain it. But do this in a gentle and respectful way." (1 Peter 3:15-16)

I am curious as to what your reaction might be to what Peter is saying to us here. What do we say to someone who asks us why we believe in Jesus, or how we can be so certain of his resurrection? As for me, I believe Peter would expect me to prepare my response. I believe he would want me to reply in confidence, yet without being argumentative. I must go over in my mind the many, many ways God has blessed me; and I need to do it until I've got it down pat. All of this takes some time and practice, doesn't it?

Personally, I would welcome the opportunity to gather with fellow believers to share how we might prepare a "defense" of our faith, as Peter seems to be encouraging us.

HERE I STAND

Roland B. Bainton was a minister, theologian, and Professor of Ecclesiastical History at the Yale Divinity School and known best perhaps for his biography of Martin Luther: Here I Stand. Time magazine, the New York Times, and the Chicago Tribune all highly praised this book, describing it as "an authoritative, unforgettable biography of a great religious leader." The central issue, of course, is Luther's bold stand against the corrupt religious practices of the medieval church and his demand that Scripture be recognized as the authority for doctrine rather than Popes and Councils. For his refusal to recant his crusade to eliminate religious abuses, he was accused of heresy and threatened with excommunication and death. Small wonder that Luther's life was filled with what he referred to as "dire plagues and despondencies."

What I found most astonishing was the means by which he sought to overcome these depressions. He shunned solitude, seeking the company of a Christian brother, a wise counselor, and undergirding himself with the fellowship of the church. He especially looked upon music as a "fair and lovely gift of God" as a remedy for his depressions.

Toward the end of the book we learn that Luther authored twenty-three hymns on his own, the best-known perhaps being what has been described as "the great battle hymn of the Reformation:" – A Mighty Fortress is our God (#504 in our red hymnal). He is said to have based this hymn on the 46th Psalm which begins "God is our refuge and strength, a very present help in trouble ..." Good News for all of us, wouldn't you agree?

You may recall my suggestion a few months back that it might be helpful if we filed away in our memory banks some of the Good News passages found in Scripture. Who knows when we might find them useful in our outreach ministry?

Luther's love of music puts one in mind of the Book of Psalms which, after all, is a collection of songs and prayers; songs of rejoicing and celebration; songs of comfort in times of trouble. I found the 103rd Psalm especially uplifting – just brimming with Good News for our memory banks. Check it out – especially verses 1-6, 10 and 12.

As Luther suggests, music, especially God's music, can be good for the soul.

THE KEYS OF THE KINGDOM

The Catholic Church has shown its dark underside with the unfortunate behavior of some of its priests and the ensuing cover-up by archbishops, cardinals, and who knows who else,

All very sad!

But the news isn't all bad. For I am here to tell you of a most lovable and saintly priest with whom I recently became acquainted. I met him in the pages of A.J. Cronin's magnificent novel, The Keys of the Kingdom. Yes, he's a fictional character, but Cronin brings him very much to life.

Francis Chisholm was a young Scot who entered the priesthood soon after the tragic loss of his father, mother, and sweetheart. He was a humble man, whose bishop saw in him a passion for pleasing God first above all else, even at the risk of incurring the displeasure of others in the clergy as well as the high-minded, wealth-seeking Catholic hierarchy.

And so it was that Francis was dispatched to the small village of Pai-tan in remote China. It was there that the good father found the keys of the kingdom.

For thirty-five years, he overcame overwhelming poverty, a vicious warlord, a killing plague, and setback after setback as he built his tiny mission from a small, makeshift chapel with a mud floor to a thriving church with a dispensary and a school for "his children."

But perhaps Father Francis's greatest challenge came from Mr. Chia, a wealthy and cultured merchant, who was very influential among Pai-tan residents.

Mr. Chia's six-year-old son, Yu, was near death due to an arm wound that had become infected. His attending physicians were three elderly Chinese, who treated him with "priceless extract of frogs' eyes." As the boy's condition worsened, Mr. Chia summoned Francis, who immediately incised the swollen arm.

Yu recovered, but Father Francis received not a word of thanks from the boy's father. Oddly, Mr. Chia did inquire of Francis how he might become a Christian. When Francis asked him if he believed, the merchant replied, "No!" Neither did he have the time for instruction in the Christian faith. Father Francis asked, "Then why are you here?" "To repay you" Mr. Chia replied. Whereupon the good father said, "You owe me nothing.

Please go."

Nonetheless, the two men enjoyed a close friendship over the next thirty years, and Father Francis's growing mission and his love of the children did not go unnoticed by Mr. Chia. When Father Francis finally received notice of his recall to Scotland, Mr. Chia expressed his hope that his friend would one day return. Francis replied, "Never! We must look forward to our meeting in the celestial hereafter." It was at this point, when a most beautiful exchange took place between the two friends, that I realized how appropriate this story would be for a Chimes article. Mr. Chia said to the Father, "I have never pondered deeply on what state lies beyond this life. But, if such a state exists, it would be very agreeable for me to enjoy your friendship there." When Father Francis did not appear to grasp his meaning, Mr. Chia continued, "My friend, I have often said that there are many religions, and each has its own gate to heaven." After a pause, he added, "Now it would appear that I have the extraordinary desire to enter by your gate." He then added, "The goodness of a religion is best judged by the goodness of its adherents. My friend, you have conquered me with your example."

A BUSINESS WORLD FAITH STORY

Corporate financial scandals involving executives of some of our largest firms have dominated news headlines for several years now. In addition, several mutual funds have been brought up on charges of fraudulent market-timing practices. On a smaller scale perhaps, some of you may have seen how pervasive corporate politics has become in some companies as employees battle their way to the top. Most of you would agree, I believe, that the business world is not where you would look first for a faith story or an example of Christian behavior.

There are exceptions, of course, and I would like to tell you a story of one of our own here at St. Paul's, and how he came to Jesus.

For many years, Frank Johnson served in a top management position for one of our nation's leading men's clothing chains. Unlike many of the executives mentioned above, who are now facing long-term prison terms for their greed at the expense of lower level employees, Frank can look back with pride on his career. But the story I want to tell you has nothing to do with decisions he made for his employer. It has everything to do with a much more important decision - a decision he made for Christ.

For some time, Frank was aware that his secretary – let's call her Jane – was away from her desk for ten or fifteen minutes early every morning. So it was with Mary, one of Jane's co- workers. Frank assumed they were on a coffee break and, sure enough, one morning he came upon them in the lunch room, each with a Bible opened before them. Being curious, he asked them what they were up to. "We're having devotions," replied Jane.

I should explain here that Frank had never been baptized. Neither could he or his lovely wife, Kathleen, be described as being steady church goers at this point in their lives. But back to the story. Frank became quite interested in what the two ladies were doing, and he asked, "If I were to begin reading the Bible, where should I start?" After a brief pause, they suggested the Gospel of Luke. He reported to his secretary the next morning and asked, "What next?" Jane recommended the book of Acts; and over the next several weeks, he read the rest of the New Testament and then went on to the Old Testament.

At some point in this process, Frank approached our former pastor, David Mangiante, and asked if he could be baptized. (Pastor M. is the person who related this story to me) However, there was one detail which the pastor omitted, of which Frank informed me later – namely, if memory served him, it was that same evening that pastor stopped by his house. So Frank not only joined the family of God, but he and K a t h le e n became very active members of St. Paul's, as well. Frank was eventually elected to Church Council where he served for many years, several as vice-president.

I thought you might enjoy this story of one of our own at St. Paul's. But let's not overlook the key roles played by Jane and Mary and their bold witness for the Lord.

YOU ARE THERE

He is not here;
He is risen.

Reflections01

In his sermon on the first Sunday after Easter, Pastor Mangiante recounted for us the amazing story of Jesus' resurrection as it is found in the twenty-fourth chapter of Luke. As he was preaching, my mind wandered a bit (through no fault of the pastor's) and a popular television program came to mind that was aired in the 1950's--You are There. Some of you who are more chronologically challenged may remember this program. Its host narrator, the respected news analyst, Walter Cronkite, invited the viewers to imagine "being there" as various historical events took place. One such event which I can still recall was the signing of the Declaration of Independence.

Jesus' resurrection was such an event, wasn't it? Arguably the greatest historical event of all time. Just imagine, if you can, how awesome it would have been to be there at the tomb with Mary

Magdelene and the other women when they found it empty, and then being told by the angels, "He is not here, but has risen." Or perhaps being one of the eleven to whom the women hurried to tell this wondrous news? What would have been your reaction? Would you have wanted proof, as Thomas did? Or would you have leaped for joy and shouted this good news to the highest rooftops? Imagine if someone were to ask you if it was really true. Could you have replied that it was – that he had risen indeed?

And imagine my surprise when Pastor Jost addressed this same theme in his sermon the following Sunday. "You are there," he said to us, there at the tomb with the others, there to hear the good news, and to hear it from one of those who had witnessed the event. How very fortunate, how blessed and privileged we are to hear this wonderful news of Jesus' resurrection, his victory over death for us, and to be among those chosen to pass it on to others?

ANGELA

We heard a beautiful faith story told during one of our Sunday morning Adult Forum sessions. It was the story of a young mother named Angela, whose son had developed a serious bone disease. And soon afterward, Angela herself was diagnosed with cancer.

As you can imagine, she was devastated, not only by her son's illness and hers, but also by the mounting medical bills she was receiving. She just couldn't handle it and didn't know to whom she could turn. Out of desperation she phoned a neighbor friend.

Well, thanks be to God, Betty dropped everything she was doing and rushed over to see what she could do for Angela. As Angela put it, "Me and her talked."

Betty listened and then she told Angela "I'm going to pray for you and your son." But Betty did a whole lot more than just pray. She went to her parishioners and, together, they organized a benefit for Angela and her son that went a long way toward helping Angela pay her medical expenses and deal with this crisis in her life.

Many needs like Angela's are being satisfied by the compassionate ministries of our pastor and our Social Ministry committee. Perhaps as much as anything else, their aid to people in need expresses our belief that St. Paul's is indeed "Blessed to be a blessing."

But you know what?! I think this makes for a nice evangelism story, too. Up to this point in her life, Angela had never been a church-going person. But she is now!

THE MARK OF ZORRO

S ome pastors like to use illustrations in their sermons to reinforce the message they are trying to convey. Sometimes an illustration might be fictional or imaginary, while other times it may be a real-life story.

One Sunday this past winter, while visiting with our daughter, Linda, and her family in Florida, Laura and I worshiped with them at Faith Lutheran Church in North Palm Beach. Their pastor, Rev. Daniel McPherson, preached on the 21st chapter of John – the story of Jesus' encounter with some of his disciples at the Sea of Galilee some eight days after his resurrection. You will recall that the disciples had just spent a frustrating night of fishing with nothing to show for it. Tired and discouraged and still with the task ahead of washing and mending their nets, they must have thought it strange when Jesus suggested they return to sea and, once again, cast their nets over the side.

But notice what happened. They obeyed! And their obedience was rewarded as they caught so many fish their nets were breaking.

But one has to ask why. Why would these men, exhausted after hours on the water, agree to go out again? Remember, they were skilled fishermen; and what was Jesus? – a carpenter? The point that Pastor Dan was trying to make was this: They trusted Jesus. They had been with him for three years and had seen what miraculous deeds he had performed. They had faith; so they humbled themselves and they obeyed him.

To illustrate these qualities that defined Jesus' disciples, Pastor Dan used a fictional, yet powerful, illustration from – of all places – Hollywood of the 1940's. Many of you may not be as chronologically challenged as I, but others of you will remember The Mark of Zorro, the adventure film starring the handsome Tyrone Power as Don Diego de la Vega, a foppish nobleman living in the Spanish Colonial era of California. There were times when Diego found it necessary to disguise himself as the fox-like Zorro to defend his people from the tyrannical despots in power at the time.

So successful was Zorro in his fight for the oppressed that reward notices of 20,000 pesos began to appear everywhere. But Zorro, with rapier in hand and astride his black stallion, Toronado, always seemed in control. Until one night an exciting chase scene finds Zorro fleeing a band of Spanish Army officers, only to find him cornered on a bridge some 20 feet above a fast-moving river. What to do? (And this is where trust and obedience come into play.)

Obviously, the only means of escape was to command his steed to leap over the suspension ropes into the cold, dark waters below. But this required great courage from the horse and rider as well.

Not a problem!

Over a period of years, Toronado had been trained by a skilled Hollywood stunt man, first making small jumps posing no danger to horse or rider, then gradually increasing the height until the horse had total trust that his trainer would never issue a command that would harm either his horse or himself. With trust, obedience and courage acquired from years of practice, Toronado was able to escape with his master, Zorro, from their evil pursuers.

Trust, faith, courage, and obedience! All of them attributes acquired by Toronado after years of teaching and practice at the hands of his master. So it was with Jesus' disciples after years with their Master.

And so it is with us as we spend our years with our Master, hearing and reading his Word and bringing his good news to others.

ASK NOT WHAT YOUR CHURCH CAN DO FOR YOU....

A panel of newscasters was asked recently what speeches they considered best among those delivered by Americans over the years. Several replied almost immediately: Abraham Lincoln's Gettysburg Address proposing that "All men are created equal". His second inaugural speech devoted to saving the Union without war was also cited, as was President Roosevelt's Day of Infamy speech following Japan's attack on Pearl Harbor on December 7, 1941.

Some panelists felt strongly that some more recent orations deserved mention, such as Martin Luther King's "I have a dream" speech and President Reagan's declaration at the Brandenburg Gate in Berlin demanding "Mr. Gorbachev, tear down this wall".

You may have some favorites of your own; but the one that stands out in my memory is President Kennedy's inspiring inaugural address on January 20, 1961: "And so, my fellow Americans, ask not what your country can do for you – ask what you can do for your country".

When given some thought, could not this same question be appropriately asked of some among us who are wondering what is going on in our congregation? Why are we doing this and no longer doing that? What lays ahead in our future?

As you may have read in Pastor's Corner column in the January Chimes and also in his recent report to Council, none of these concerns has escaped his attention. (Both of these documents can be found on the counter as you enter the Narthex). Pastor has designated seventeen dates and locations in and around our church where those of you with questions or concerns can be heard. He wants to listen to you and has offered you several opportunities to voice your opinions. Hopefully you attended one of these meetings, as he plans to address these issues at the February 22nd Annual Meeting. Hope to see you present then.

If you read your Chimes, you will notice that some new steps have already been taken.

Religious Education classes began on January 31st - 9:45 to 10:45 am – this in response to the pleas of many for Sunday morning religious education. Thankfully some have already volunteered to lead/facilitate these sessions. Perhaps we'll see you there. Also First Communion classes were offered on January 22nd and January 26th. (see page 13 of your January Chimes). In addition, Lutheran Men in Mission discussions began on January 15th and will continue on the third Saturday of each month.

We need to keep one thing in mind: Pastor Jost will need a lot of help to satisfy everyone's needs. He cannot do it alone. Thankfully, some have already stepped forward and expressed their willingness to pitch in and help. How about you?

We might all do well to take President Kennedy's inaugural address remarks to heart and apply them to ourselves: "And so my fellow Christians, ask not what your church can do for you – ask instead what you can do for your church". Paul's remarks in his letter to the Romans may help us with this. (Romans 12:1-2; 12:6; and 14:17-19)

THE CARPENTER'S APPRENTICE

I believe that we benefit from learning how great men and women have lived their lives for Christ and mankind. Of course, we may read about many such persons in Scripture; but aren't there others from more recent times whom we can and should honor for the way they lived?

You may recall in one of the Chimes issues my mention of Corrie ten Boom as one whose life has had a most positive impact during and following her imprisonment by the Nazis. Now I would like to propose to you the name of another whose life of public service and witness to our Lord deserves our utmost esteem. His name is Jimmy Carter.

When he sought the presidency in 1976, he did not get my vote, and I was not particularly impressed with his term in office. But, what do I know? My opinion of him remained pretty much unchanged until recently when my sister-in-law sent me a copy of his spiritual biography, The Carpenter's Apprentice.

By the time I finished the book, I was of the firm belief that this man was one of the finest statesmen and humanitarians of our time. History may not recognize him as one of our greater presidents, but his life of public service and Christian witness since leaving office far surpasses, in my opinion, that of any other former president.

His legacy as president is pretty much a matter of record, but let me tell you a little of what kind of man I have learned he is.

Jimmy Carter has been described as a warrior for peace, traveling worldwide to prevent military confrontations in such places as Haiti and North Korea. At his Carter Center in Atlanta, the International Negotiating Network (INN) monitors conflicts in Bosnia, Somalia, Angola, Armenia, Azerbaijan, Burma, Cyprus, Kosovo, Liberia, Macedonia, Sudan and Zaire.

The center has helped to upgrade agricultural and environmental conditions in Third World countries. It also addresses such issues as basic human rights, including adequate food, shelter, access to medical services, poverty and inadequate housing in urban communities.

Among his prestigious humanitarian and peace awards are the Fulbright Prize for International Peace Keeping, the Albert Schweitzer Prize for Humanitarianism, and the Martin Luther King Jr. Nonviolent Peace Prize.

Mr. Carter's private life has also been devoted to making lives better for others, especially the poor. Since 1984, he and his wife, Rosalynn, have been faithful workers for Habitat for Humanity, often trying to limit media contact while, at the same time, setting a work pace matched by few other volunteers.

As often as possible when he and Rosalynn are at home in Plains, Georgia, Jimmy Carter teaches adult education classes at Maranatha Baptist Church. He also takes his turn mowing the grounds, and he actively recruits new church members. His has been a ministry of hospitality that promotes three messages: You are welcome here – We believe that Jesus is the Son of God, Savior and model for our individual lives – And the best way to serve Jesus is by serving others.

His prayer life is "praying without ceasing." He asks God to let him do what is best so that his life might be meaningful. Rosalynn believes strongly in sharing her life with her husband and noted that, as her husband walked through the Rose Garden to his oval office in the White House at 5:30 or 6:00 o'clock in the morning, his prayer was from Psalm 19: "Let the words of my mouth and the meditations of my heart be acceptable in Thy sight, O Lord, my strength and my redeemer."

Jimmie Carter believes that Christ would define a successful life as one of humility, service, suffering if necessary, and a life of compassion for "unlovable people."

Time and space are not adequate here to do justice to this man and his life. You really have to read the book to understand his strong spiritual nature and his dogged determination to make his life count for the cause of Christ. He is truly a great human being and a devoted servant of God, a man who has used his considerable talents and energy to make the most of his life as well as to improve the lives of others around the world.

JESUS' HEALING MINISTRIES

When I was a boy, it was my Dad's habit to head for the living room after dinner to listen to the latest newscasts on the radio. One of his favorite newscasters was Gabriel Heater who often began his newscast with a hearty "I've got GOOD NEWS TONIGHT." He would then launch into the latest reports of allied advances coming from the battle fronts of Europe, North Africa, and the South Pacific.

Well, I've got some good news of my own to report, especially for those of you who have had me in your thoughts and prayers these past weeks after a pretty serious head injury. No pain, no dizziness, and vital signs are good, all due in large part to your prayers, Jesus' healing, excellent medical care, and some darn good home care from my wife, Laura, and her friend, Midy. I have to wonder: With all the sickness in the world, including many of our friends here at St. Paul's, Why Me?? Why am I so fortunate? I've done a lot of thinking about this, and I'm convinced that, yes, it is your prayers and God's response to them. But I believe there's more to it than that. How about trust in God's healing? I confess that trust has not always been one of my strong suits. But I'm trying to do better. I'm trying to just leave it all in God's hands.

One day after returning home from the hospital, my good friend, Clyde Zarkos, paid me a visit. As he was leaving, he left with me a packet of booklets which he and his wife, Jerry, shared with hospital patients whom they visited during their more than twenty years of hospital care- giving ministry. One of the booklets was titled "The Healing Power of the Twenty Third Psalm.

What a Godsend! Phrase by phrase, the writer, Charles Allen, casts his light upon the calming words of the Psalm. St. Paul does much the same thing in his letter to the Philippians: "If we have faith, we need not worry about tomorrow." Each phrase of the Psalm is examined beautifully.

Just as the Good Shepherd tends to the wounds his sheep incurred while grazing amid the briars and thorns, so our Good Shepherd tends and heals our wounds. Good News!

·All of this puts me in mind of Matthew's accounts in his Gospel of the thousands healed by Jesus during his ministry. As you read these events, you will notice how often faith had much to do with healing. Matthew 8: 5-10 -the Centurion's servant; Matthew 8: 28-32 – the demoniacs; Matthew 9:2 – the paralytic; Matthew 9:18-26 – the synagogue Leader's daughter, and the woman suffering from hemorrhages for twelve years: Matthew 9: 27-29 the two blind men;

Matthew 9:32-33 – the mute; Matthew 12:9-13 – the man with the withered hand; Mathew 14:34-36 – the sick in Gennesaret; Matthew 15: 21-28 –the Canaanite woman's daughter; Matthew 15:29-31–the many people of Galilee;; Matthew 17: 14-18 – the epileptic boy. And of course, many of these good news miracles are recorded in the other Gospels, as well

When Jesus' disciples asked him to teach them how to pray (Luke11:1-4), he answers by teaching them (and us) his Lord's Prayer. And, of course, we always have his promise ... "ask, and it will be given you." (v9). But, as we see in many of these healing stories in Matthew, Jesus also looks for us to pray in faith.

CALLED TO BE EVANGELICAL

As I was leafing through some papers in my evangelism file, I came across this article written several years ago by Martin E. Marty. It appeared as part of an ELCA bulletin insert entitled "Called to be Evangelical:"

A sage Christian thinker once said that for years he had preached: "You've got to love!" Late in life the word of the gospel reached him, and he learned that he should have been saying "You get to love!" God empowers us to love – gives us the gift of loving.

Think of this statement: "You've got to be evangelical!" That kind of command could mean any of a number of things. It might mean that we should get involved with mass evangelism, go to big rallies, and admire revivalists. Or to some it might mean that we've got to go to airports, hand out tracts, grasp people by the lapels and tell them how we are born again.

The fact that good people do those things is not the issue here. The important thing is that we hear a promise, not a command: "You get to be evangelical!"

But, what is "getting to be evangelical" about?

In a simple sense, it could mean that we "get" to be members of a church body with that word in its title: The Evangelical Lutheran Church in America. This is a beautiful name for a promising church; but it can also be only a name.

Secondly, we "get to be evangelical" could mean that we are part of a movement where people hear and realize the Good News of what God does in Jesus to save a sinful humanity – including you within that humanity. That's better than just being a member of something.

Now comes a third reality: We "get to be evangelical" in a sense that we are privileged to share the Gospel, the Good News of what God has done for us in Jesus Christ. That means that we can forgive others because God has forgiven us for Jesus' sake. Likewise, because we know that God cares for us, we can care for those who are hurt or oppressed.

"Getting to be evangelical" means that, whether we are bold or shy, eloquent or mumbly, courageous or timid, we get to invite others to be a part of what God is doing.

Inviting means making it easier for others to come with us to God's house. It means having us put into words the change Christ brings into our lives. It includes the idea that we get a chance to put our faith to work, that faith becomes "active in love." We can think of all this as a command; but we get to think of it as a promise. We get to be evangelical. God makes it possible.

Martin E. Marty

Our ELCA Bishop, E. Roy Riley at the time, had this to say about Mr. Marty's article:

What a difference it makes to think of the church not as a command, but a promise being fulfilled! Think of the power of a New Church whose people could see the mission God places before them as a gift, and not as an imposition or burden! To know that it is a precious opportunity to, in Christ's name and in partnership with him, to serve; to feed the hungry and shelter the homeless. To know that it is a privilege to stand in Christ's name for justice for those who are oppressed. To know that it is an enormous honor to be entrusted with the Good News of a Savior who is Christ the Lord….Good News to be shared with all humankind!

We GET to be partners in mission with our Lord Jesus Christ. We GET to be the church because God calls us; and then, empower us with the Holy Spirit, with the resources we need, and with promises to which God is always faithful. God makes it all possible. The church is a gift.... a "get to" long before it is a "got to." And church only becomes a "got to" when I am so overwhelmed with God's grace to me in Jesus Christ.... the enormity of that gift....that finally I can do nothing less than to be the evangelical good and faithful steward I am called to be. Together We Do More!

Pastor E. Roy Riley, Jr.

COURAGE REVISITED

Courage is a virtuous quality often displayed on the battle field or on the seas. also by fire fighters risking their lives to save others, and by astronauts thrust into space to make known the unknown.

And let us not overlook the scores of Christians who have demonstrated courage of a spiritual nature throughout history— Stephen, for example, the first Christian martyr, who was stoned to death for his courageous witness of Jesus to the elders and scribes. And what courage it took for Martin Luther to denounce the sale of indulgences and for refusing to recant his ninety-five theses when brought before the Emperor and church officials at the Diet of Worms. And Dietrich Boenhoeffer, the young Lutheran pastor who publicly repudiated the Nazis during WW11, worked for the defeat of Hitler, and lived a life of discipleship only to be hanged for his courageous efforts just days before the war's end.

There may be others who come to mind. What about the apostle Paul and, of course, Jesus' disciples who went forth to preach the Gospel in such far-off lands as Italy, Spain, India, Mesopotamia, Persia and Britain. What courage they displayed knowing full well what awaited them – persecution, flogging, and for some, a grizzly death.

And so it has been in modern times as we contemplate the spiritual courage of missionaries who offered their lives for Christ in such remote places as China, the Philippines and the jungles of Africa and Brazil.

Many women, as well, have exhibited great courage. A friend suggested to me Esther, the beautiful woman of Jewish parentage who saved the Hebrew nation from annihilation at the hands of Haman; and Mary, upon hearing the angel Gabriel's news that she was to conceive and give birth to the Son of the Most High, and then summoning the courage to reply, "Here am I, servant of the Lord; let it be according to your word." And also, the prostitute, Rahab, who courageously sheltered the two Israelite spies at Jericho.

There are others of course -- Corrie ten Boom, for instance, and her sister, Betsy, who so courageously preached the Gospel to fellow prisoners at the notorious German prison camp at Ravensbruck, Germany.

We are taught that we are to complete the work that Jesus and his disciples began – to go forth and proclaim the Good News. Does this mean that literally we are to give up our lives for him as did many of his followers? What's your take on this? I don't know; but, at a bare minimum, I have to think God expects us to tell others what he has done for us and what joy awaits us when we put him first in our lives.

GOOD NEWS! - WHERE TO SEEK IT, AND FIND IT

While walking up our driveway one morning, I opened our local newspaper to catch the news headlines. What I found was very upsetting. There, covering almost the entire front page was a photo of a rather nice-looking young man clad in an orange prison jump suit. The adjacent column reported his brutal rape and murder of a young woman in a nearby town. I thought to myself: Do we really need this kind of news?

A few days later, while Laura was preparing supper, I turned on the five o'clock news. The first ten minutes were devoted to three murders – one by machete –another was drug- related – and the third was an account of a five year old girl who was accidentally gunned down during a Philadelphia street drive-by shooting.

Bad news! Bad news! Bad news!

I was disgusted. Oddly I was also curious. Was it really true what some say about the media, that they really try to appeal to the public by reporting the sensational?

So, for the next few days I made it my business to study the news headlines and feature stories being reported. Here is some of what I found.

* Missing man's body found in Manchester.
* The Confession – McGreevy discusses his coming out book with Oprah.
* Ex Ramsey suspect to fight porn charges.

Enough already!

By now I suspect that some of you have a pretty good idea where I'm going with this.

Is there any place where we can find some good news?

Well, the good news is that there is good news to be found. How about if we just turn off to our TV's, our radios, and our daily tabloids and turn on to our Bibles, our Church, Jesus Christ, and the good news he brings us – love and hope – mercy and forgiveness _ and so much more. Just a few selections from Scripture:

* "The Lord is my shepherd, I shall not want ..." Psalm 23
* "He is not here, but has risen..." Luke 24:5
* "Do not let your hearts be troubled ... in my Father's house there are many dwelling places ... and if I go to prepare a place for you, I will come again and take you to myself ..." Luke 14: 1-3
* "For all who are led by the Spirit of God are children of God ... you have received a spirit of adoption ... we are children of God, and if children of God, then heirs, heirs of God and joint heirs with Christ ..." Romans 8: 14-17
* "For God so loved the world that he gave his only Son ..." (I think you know the rest) John 3:16

Sadly, there are many who don't know where to find this good news. But we can tell them, can't we? We can invite them to come to church with us – or to Bible study – places where they will be treated to some really sensational news – the good news of Jesus Christ.

THANK GOD WE HAVE AN EMPTY TOMB

These are the poignant, soul-stirring words spoken by Peter to close his First Easter sermon. No, I'm not referring to Peter, the Apostle. It's another man called Peter to whom I would like to draw your attention. This Peter, also a faithful disciple of Christ, died in 1949 at the age of 46. It's unlikely that any of you baby boomers or gen-exers have ever heard of Peter Marshall, a man who was revered by thousands who heard him preach. His was not a long life; but it was a life that took him from boyhood in poverty-stricken Scotland to a life of spiritual wealth, culminating with his appointment as Chaplain of the United States Senate.

It was this Peter whose life was beautifully chronicled by his wife, Catherine, in her book, A Man Called Peter, and later in film with the same title. She believed that it was in the pulpit that the mantle of greatness fell upon him and that his picturesque style exhibited the enthusiasm of a little boy who had just made the most important discovery in the world and couldn't wait to share it with anyone who would listen.

And thousands did listen. It was said that people standing in lines surrounding Peter Marshall's church each Sunday, waiting patiently to hear him preach, were a familiar sight to Washingtonians.

One of his sermons had a life-changing impact on a young woman who heard him for the first time. She described it this way: By the time my friend and I got inside the church there were no seats left except the stairs leading to the balcony. The music was lovely. Then the man in the pulpit began to preach. As Dr. Marshall spoke of the resurrection, the full meaning came into my heart for the first time." She later wrote him a letter thanking him for introducing her to the One who had brought joy back into her life.

Yet another lady put it this way, "Peter was nearly my idol and would have been if he hadn't stepped out of the way and let me glimpse the Savior. I met Him through Peter Marshall."

Peter was heard to have said more than once that no man could look at Jesus and remain the same.

After his untimely death, Catherine found in her possession ninety-six Easter manuscripts from eighteen years and four months of preaching. Many of his sermons and prayers are beautifully recorded in her book, Mr. Jones, Meet Your Master.

But it's another of her books that I would like to recommend to you, The First Easter, a vivid portrayal of Christ's passion and the profound effect it had on the impulsive Simon who was to become Peter, the Rock. Catherine describes what she considers "the loveliest record of God dealing with a penitent sinner." As Simon and his Master meet on the beach following the resurrection. Three times the question, "Simon, lovest Thou Me?" and three times the answer, "Yes, Lord, Thou knowest that I love Thee." For each of Simon's earlier denials, Christ now offers His disciple three opportunities to pledge his love for his Master and, in this manner, make everything all right again.

On the very last page Peter reminds us of Jesus' good news: "Because I live, you shall live also." Thank God we have an empty tomb.

THE GOOD NEWS AND HOW TO SHARE IT

In his book titled How Will They Hear if we Don't listen? Pastor Ronald Johnson states "Anytime the Gospel is shared with another (and it must be done verbally) .... confrontation takes place." He claims that evangelism always involves a verbal witness to the facts and demands of the Gospel.

What's your take on this? Can we only share the Good News by engaging unbelievers in verbal conversation?

My first reaction was: No way! Haven't we been taught that we proclaim Christ by the way we live? What about when we feed the hungry – when we care for the sick – when we "do unto others what we would have them do unto us" – or when we simply go to church?

But as I thought about this, it occurred to me that most, if not all, of Jesus' ministry was done verbally. He spoke the parables. He spoke of his "living water" to the Samaritan woman at the well. He preached to thousands throughout Galilee, Judea, Samaria. So did Paul and Jesus' disciples as they traveled the world as it was then known. The New Testament is replete with stories of Christians proclaiming Jesus to the world. Peter's Pentecost sermon that added more than three thousand to the Church, -- his journey to Caesarea to speak to Cornelius, his relatives and friends – and Philip as he helped the Ethiopian Eunuch understand what he was reading. All of this seems to lend credence to Pastor Johnson's claim that we are to share the Gospel with others verbally.

But I'm still not fully convinced that it's the only way to reach unbelievers. Why can't it be done with the written word? After all, the very word of God is written for us. It's right there in the Bible. We can read it – and re-read it. We can study it and discuss it and meditate upon it.

Similarly, Paul didn't only preach the word. He wrote letters to the churches he had established. So did Peter and John and others. In the third Gospel Luke wrote in his very first chapter "After investigating everything carefully, I decided to write an orderly account of the events …." He wrote to us of the truth.

So where do we stand on this issue. Must our witness to others be verbal only? Or can we reach out with the written word that teaches how to live Christ-like lives? As for me, I'm going to try to do as many of our politicians often do. I'm going to come down right in the middle. Let's do it both ways. Let's use every opportunity that God gives us to bring Christ to others.

A DAY IN JUNE

" And what is so rare as a day in June?"
So begins perhaps one of the more familiar poems written by James Russell Lowell, a popular American Romantic poet of the 19th century. I'm really not into poetry that much, but this poem struck a chord in me, so much so that I felt inspired to put my thoughts into this article written for the August, 2006 Chimes, the monthly newsletter published here at St. Paul's. It's one of my favorites.

. While relaxing with a book on our back porch, I sensed a certain peace and calm.

My reading was interrupted; so I set my book aside for a while and just marveled at what I saw and heard. With the rustling of the leaves in the trees and the birds chattering to one another, it was almost idyllic -- like having my own little private aviary.

It sounds pretty corny, doesn't it? But I don't care. I wondered to myself what could possibly compare: perhaps a walk on a lonely beach at sunset – or sitting on the end of a pier at night with a full moon reflecting on the lake. Or even the peace one feels when holding an infant child in your arms as it nods off to sleep.

Some of you may have experienced your own rare day in June. I hope so. We should all be alert for special moments like these so that we can put everything aside for an hour or so and just enjoy God's magnificent creation.

He is so good! Especially when we realize that rare days like these are his gifts to us – free of charge, just like his grace.

One almost feels a need to ask what we can do in return. But aren't we taught that it's not about what we can do – that it's all about what God has already done for us?

Pastor Stoner often tells us during our Wednesday morning Bible Study that we must respond to what God has done for us by praising him for his countless blessings.

And how blessed we are to have such beautiful music to sing God's praises like How Great Thou Art, which opens: "O Lord My God, when I in awesome wonder" consider all the works thy hand hath made …"

Go ahead! If you have a hymnal at home, sing it through – all four verses. Nobody's listening – except maybe God.

As I read what I have written, I realize once again that it's not all that easy for me to relate these thoughts to evangelism. But I do believe that, as we bring others to worship with us, they will feel the same passion that we feel when we sing these hymns of praise.

And they, too, may come to understand better just how great their God is.

UNDERSTANDING SCRIPTURE

Do you ever wonder to yourself if you are living your life the way God wants you to? I mean completely – in thought, word and deed. Tough question!? Here's another one.

Do you believe that you have reached your full potential as a Christian? Or, putting it another way, are you really using all of the gifts that God has given you – your time, your talents, and your treasures -- to serve Him and others?

Some of you may be able to answer "yes" to one or perhaps both of these questions.

I can't. It helps me some when I remember that no one is perfect. And it helps even more when I am reminded that it's not so much about what we do for God as it is about what God has already done for us. But does that mean that we don't even have to try to respond to his love and grace? I don't think so.

Many of our friends at St. Paul's are trying by looking to Bible study as a means of learning about God. They are finding that reading God's word is one thing. Understanding it is quite another.

If we really want to live our lives for Christ, what better way than to let Him teach us how?

I recently asked this question of those in the study class that I attend: "How would you say that Bible study is helping you?" Here's what some had to say.

* I'm beginning to find out how little I understand in the Bible when I read it alone at home.

* It helps so much to hear pastor explain something. But, you know, I think we learn from each other, too.
* I believe that it's becoming easier for me to speak more openly about Jesus.
* It challenges my understanding of the Bible.
* I'm learning what I need to do to be a disciple of Jesus.
* I enjoy just being together like this...the chance to really get to know someone with whom I've only been acquainted before.
* I like the faith stories some of you have told.

As we adjourned after class one day, one of my friends remarked, "wasn't that terrific!" Another said, "I wonder why more people don't come." I thought: Perhaps some might be reluctant to come because they know so little about God's word and feared others might think less of them for this. To anyone who feels this way I say, "Nonsense! It is you who would benefit the most. Come and see for yourself – even if you just come and listen. You would be most welcome."

There are several Bible studies scheduled each week from which you can choose. You'll find them listed in the church bulletin every Sunday; or check with the church office.

So, ask yourself if you have the time. You just might find it will become the best time of the week for you.

IMAGINATION....ONE OF GOD'S MOST PRECIOUS GIFTS

A friend of mine once asked me if I had ever tried to imagine what heaven will be like. Judging from my puzzled expression he must have realized that he had caught me by surprise. So he asked "Who will we see? Do you think we'll be able to recognize our families and friends?" I shrugged and replied "I suppose so."

Not to be put off by my apparent lack of interest, he continued:. "I was thinking about this just yesterday, and my imagination really took over. Listen! It was a really far out experience."

"All of a sudden it was as though I was being lifted up - alone amid some bright, fluffy clouds. And there was music that I could only describe as – heavenly. Could that be what was happening? Was I on my way to heaven? Then just above appeared a man clad in a white robe, and he was beckoning me upward toward him. It was almost like he was expecting me; and I wondered to myself if this could be St. Peter. He extended a warm welcome and, putting his arm around my shoulder, he ushered me through a gate into our Savior's heavenly home.

What a sight! So radiant and beautiful! And I could hear music – lovely, angelic music.

I found myself being led toward a huge chamber filled with angels and others whom I took to be saints – all of them singing joyful, alleluia praises to our King. Awesome doesn't begin to describe what I was experiencing. And then gradually the throng ahead began to part; and there was Jesus sitting upon his throne and looking just as I had imagined as a child.

He was smiling and then he, too, beckoned me to come to Him. Tears of gladness filled my eyes as I kneeled before Him. And then He said "Welcome home, my son." He reached out and touched me on the forehead and blessed me.

With that, Peter took me by the arm and led me away. "Wait," I protested. "I want to thank Him for all that He has done for me – for His life and His teachings - and for His suffering and His death – and for His victory over death." Peter then explained "There will be time for that. He has heard your prayers of thanksgiving many times over; and now you will be with Him forever, just as He promised. Come along now. There are others waiting anxiously to see you."

Then just ahead he pointed to a small group of five (saints perhaps) who were running toward us, smiling with arms extended in greeting. Sure enough, there was Mom and Dad, my brother and both my sisters. Hugs and kisses! Wow! And tears aplenty! What joy!

St. Peter waited patiently until we had our fill of one another and then whispered to me "Come along, my friend, there is one other who asked if he might have a moment with you."

"Who could that be" I wondered aloud. "You shall see." And soon he directed me toward an elderly man sitting on a bench just ahead. When he recognized my host and me, he quickly rose and hurried toward us. Holding me at arm's length he said "You may not remember me, but my name is Bill, and I was a hospital roommate of one of your church friends whom you once visited in Mt. Holly. I remember that, before leaving, you prayed with him and left him with a small booklet. I was moved by the obvious love you had for one another. After you left I asked him about the booklet, and he handed it to me explaining that it was a devotional booklet.

At the time I wasn't what you would call a religious man but, as I read the booklet, he could see that I was interested. The two of us talked at some length about Jesus, and he told me all that He had done for us.

"After my release from the hospital I began going to church; and over time Jesus and I have become fast friends. Thanks to you my life was changed forever."

"We hugged, and I thanked him for his beautiful story. Often I had wondered if I had ever made a difference in anyone's life. When I told him this, he smiled and said "Well look what you've done for me."

I knew, of course, that it was the Holy Spirit who had brought Jesus to Bill (or is it the other way around; I never could get that straight); and that I was just kind of an intermediary. But it was a grand feeling just the same."

All of this, of course, is just a product of my friend's imagination. His joyous account of reuniting with loved ones may not conform with what Paul tells us in 1 Corinthians 15

– that we will be changed and raised in spiritual bodies. But I have to think that Paul would not take strong exception to my friend's vivid imagination. No doubt your image of heaven is quite different; but one thing is for sure: Heaven is sure to be infinitely more glorious than any of us can imagine.

A CHRISTIAN PROFILE

One of the books I bought at our last used book sale was quite small – only 112 pages. It is titled, Love Abounds – A Profile of Harry Denman – a Modern Disciple, and it portrays a remarkable man who lived every day for his Lord and, in so doing, made Jesus known to thousands of people around the world. I would like to add his name to others I have read and written about in previous issues of Chimes as being another we should honor for their strong Christian influence over the past 100 years.

Harry Denman served as General Secretary of the Board of Evangelism for the Methodist Church during the last 25 years of his career. His evangelistic missions have taken him to every state in the nation many times. He has traveled worldwide sharing Christ while walking the roads of Pakistan and India, sleeping in their beds, eating their curry and rice. He has been to Brazil, Scandinavia, Malaysia, Korea, Cuba, Rhodesia, Katanga, staying in their homes, adopting their customs, loving them – and always witnessing for Christ. Harry believed strongly that evangelism should be the first business of the church.

What makes this man so exceptional, however, is the manner in which he lives every day for his Lord – how he manages to avail himself of every opportunity to speak of Christ to everyone he encounters – taxi drivers, waitresses, airline stewardesses, men and women sitting beside him in railway stations or airports. He was expert at turning a conversation to God. He might ask a taxi driver if he had to work on Sunday, what church he belonged to, did he have any children, and did they go to Sunday school. And he would always ask them to pray for him. Before saying "good-bye" he would ask a person's address so that he could write a letter after he returned to his hotel room or his office. Often he enclosed a book of prayers or a Bible. And he would always repeat in his letter his hope that they would pray for him, it being his desire that prayer would become a regular part of their daily devotional life, just as it was to him.

Denman's devotional life was cultivated by copying scripture passages he was reading. He believed this helped him understand better what God was saying to him. He prayed constantly everywhere he went -- in airports, people's homes, restaurants, and places of business. While traveling with a pastor friend on a preaching mission to the Holy Land, their car became mired in mud. While others struggled to free the car, Harry disappeared to find a place to pray. Soon he was discovered a short distance away praying the Lord's Prayer: "Our Father ... Thy will be done - through me, through me..." And he always prayed "in Jesus' name", taking this admonition most seriously.

I have recorded here only that which most impressed me about this extraordinary Christian; but there is a great deal more to this man. Anyone wishing to read more about him is most welcome to borrow my book.

CHRISTIAN STRONG

I t was just over a year ago that Super Storm Sandy slammed into the Jersey shoreline, killing more than a hundred and wreaking havoc on homes and businesses in its path. Despite the gallant efforts of first responders, some have described Sandy's impact as being even worse than Katrina's some five years ago. In recognition of those who responded to the needs of homeowners and business persons who were victimized by the storm, Governor Christie coined the phrase – JERSEY STRONG – stronger than the storm itself.

It was just a few months later that we also witnessed the horrific terrorist bombing that killed and maimed many innocent observers at the Boston Marathon. Thanks to the prompt response of spectators, emergency medical personnel, and the police, many lives were saved, and the terrorists were quickly brought to justice. So intense was the reaction throughout the region to this atrocity that BOSTON STRONG became the rallying cry of people throughout the region.

Even as we read Scripture, we learn of first responders during biblical times. Our Father in heaven responded to the needs of all sinners when he gave away his only Son to die for our sins. (John 3:16)

So it was for Peter and Paul and a host of disciples who responded to Jesus' command to go and make disciples of all the nations, each of them knowing full well the persecution and peril that awaited them at the hands of rulers and unbelievers. (Mt. 10: 16-21; 28)

Jesus once told his disciples, "I tell you the truth, anyone who is in me will do the same works I have done, and even greater works, because I am going to be with the Father." He went on to say they could ask for anything in his name, and he would do it. (John 14:12-14)) My first reaction to all of this was - No way! No one could do what he had done during the past three years of his ministry on earth.

But, as I thought about this and read in my Bible commentary what some scholars have said about this, it became clear to me that as a group – a band of brothers, if you will, the twelve could, indeed, surpass all that Jesus had done.

After all, they had completed a three year apprenticeship with him. They were now journeyman teachers and healers; and they had the guidance and power of Jesus' advocate, the Holy Spirit, to turn to in Jesus' absence.

That same Spirit now abides in us, and we are promised that he will give us the words to say and the courage to say them, as we continue to grow God's kingdom. Let's not forget! Millions of Jesus' disciples have gone before us, sharing the Gospel and growing God's kingdom.

As members of Christ's church, together, we also can do great things, like helping to make the world CHRISTIAN STRONG.

A THIRTEENTH DISCIPLE

Have you ever wondered what it would have been like living in biblical times? Imagine, if you can, residing in a town like Capernaum, or any other of the towns bordering, or close by, the Sea of Galilee.

It was largely in this region where John the Baptist was heard proclaiming the arrival of Jesus, the long-awaited Messiah. And, of course, it was there that Jesus began his ministry of teaching, healing, and performing miracles. And it was there, one day, as the Baptist was chatting with two of Jesus' followers, he declared," Look, There is the Lamb of God." When they asked Jesus where he was staying, he replied," Come and see." And they did. "And they stayed with him the rest of the day" (John 1:35; 39)

If we fast forward a few weeks, we find that Jesus has assembled a group of twelve followers whom we have come to know as disciples – a few fishermen, a tax collector, of all people, and several others. None of them were scholars. Neither did they possess any apparent talents to do what Jesus had in mind for them. All were pretty ordinary people, not too unlike most of us. But Jesus knew he would have them all to himself for the next three years, preparing them for a remarkable career change.

Scripture tells us that God knew us before we were born; and that everything is possible through Him. Could God have great plans for us, just as he did for the original twelve? I believe He has. Why else would He have left us with the Holy Spirit? When we welcome Him into our hearts, he can teach us, lead us, and empower us to make disciples. And Jesus himself promises to be with us to the end of the age.

So, here's my question for you: What if, one day, Jesus decided to add a thirteenth disciple, just to make certain he had enough. And let's say he took notice of you as he passed by, and then invited you to join his small band of trainees. Could you have mustered up the courage and done what Andrew and John did here — just drop everything and join up? Or would you have responded perhaps as I might: "Can I have a week or so to think it over?"

In truth, when Jesus left us with the Holy Spirit, He has already given us all we need, hasn't He? With the Spirit's guidance and leadership, we are empowered to fulfill our Lord's Great Commission to "go and make disciples...."

CHRIST'S MOST POWERFUL WITNESS

S ome of you may agree with me and, of course, some of you may not; but when it comes to gospel music, my favorite is the Bill and Gloria Gaither Gospel Hour. I love their music, not just for the beautiful sound of their family of musicians, but for the utter joy they exhibit while singing God's praises.

One night recently, while surfing our cable channels to find out when the Gaithers might be scheduled, I chanced upon a minister who was speaking of witnessing. So I stayed with him for a few minutes.

He invited a few of his more willing listeners to come forth and speak briefly of their faith and their relationship with Jesus. And then he asked his vast audience a question: "Who, in your opinion, was the most overpowering witness for Jesus ever?"

It was getting on toward midnight, and I still had to brush my teeth and say my prayers; so I taped the rest of the show, turned out the lights and headed for bed. But, as I lay down, the minister's question kept nagging me for an answer.

Might it have been John the Baptist? After all, it was he, was it not, who, at Jesus' baptism was the first to proclaim Christ as the Messiah? And I believe it was either Billy Sunday or Billy Graham who has been referred to as the greatest evangelist since John the Baptist. Both, of course, were prominent evangelists of the twentieth century.

I believe Jesus himself might feel strongly his dear friend and disciple, Mary Magdalene, is worthy of consideration. It was she who announced to the world on Easter morning that He, indeed, had risen from the dead.

Others might contend that Jesus' disciple, Peter, is justifiably worthy of mention. Yes, Peter, the "rock" upon whom Jesus would build his church. Luke tells us in the second chapter of Acts of Peter's powerful sermon on Pentecost when some three thousand people were baptized and added to the church.

And, yes, what about Paul? Was it not he who established so many of the churches during his missionary travels throughout Asia, Syria, Galatia, Macedonia and Rome, while everywhere enduring all manor of hostility and punishment, and even imprisonment?

And so it was with Jesus' disciples who, empowered by the Holy Spirit at Pentecost, courageously testified throughout the world of their Master with whom they had lived and followed both before and after his resurrection. You know, in the fourteenth chapter of John, Jesus told his disciple, Philip that anyone who believes in him will do the same works that He had done, and "even more works."(v.12) Can you imagine that? His remark, most likely, was intended for his disciples' ears; but he did say "anyone who believes in him." Might He have been speaking to us, as well?

You may feel there are others worthy of mention; but let me now move on to the TV minister – (I'm sorry, but I never caught his name) – and see how he answers his own provocative question: "The most powerful witness of Jesus Christ" he replies "is none other than His Father in heaven" – the Father whose voice announced from heaven at Jesus' Baptism "This is my Son, the Beloved, in whom I am well-pleased." (Matthew 3:17) – the Son who would soon overcome Satan in the wilderness and begin a ministry of teaching and healing that would prove to the world that He was the long-awaited Messiah. I'm sorry, but I never caught his name. His reply; "The most powerful witness of Jesus Christ is none other than His Father in heaven – the Father whose voice announced from heaven at Jesus' baptism "This is my Son, the Beloved, in whom I am well- pleased." (Matthew 3:17) - the Son who would soon bring Satan to his knees in the wilderness and begin a ministry of teaching and healing that would prove to the world that He was the long- awaited Messiah.

THE GREEN PAPER BAG

A head cold and mild fever had made sleeping difficult for almost a week. So, when the doorbell rang on Monday morning, I simply ignored it. When it rang again, I carefully parted the curtain to see who it might be. A woman was standing on the porch steps and she was holding a green paper bag. It took a minute or two before she returned to her car, and it appeared that she was writing something. She then retraced her steps and, for a third time, rang the doorbell again. Persistent lady, I thought to myself.

Finally, getting no answer, she turned and left.

When I was certain that she was out of sight, I opened the door and, sure enough, there on my doorstep was the green paper bag. I retrieved it and set it on my kitchen table.

Later that morning, as I was reading the paper over a cup of coffee, I took notice of the bag. Curious, I peeked inside and discovered that it contained a Bible, a few other things, and a bag of cookies which appeared to be homemade.

The news was mostly bad, so I set the paper aside and began flipping through the pages of the Bible. And there was the lady's hand-written note. I noticed the letterhead: Saint Paul's Evangelical Lutheran Church – the very same church that I had visited the day before. The note read: "Sorry I missed you. I just stopped by to say that it was nice having you worship with us yesterday. Please come again when you can. You are always welcome at Saint Paul's."

Wasn't that nice, I thought to myself. Maybe I will go back.

She said that I was welcome; and everyone I met after the service seemed so pleasant.

As it happened, the Bible laid open on the table to chapter nine on page 993. It had been a long time since I had opened a Bible – years in fact. So I read a few lines from a section headed Jesus Has Pity on People. One verse in particular caught my attention: "He said to his disciples 'A large crop is in the fields, but there are only a few workers. Ask the Lord in charge of the harvest to send out workers to bring it in." Could it be that the lady on my door step was one of his workers – and that I was part of his harvest? It almost seemed so.

So you see, the story has a happy ending. The sick lady with the cold did return to Saint Paul's and has now made it her own church home. And she even brought a friend with her.

If you haven't guessed by now, this is a fictional story. Yep! I made it up. But it could be true, couldn't it? In fact, something like this probably has happened before – perhaps several times. It's really not all that hard to believe, especially when you take into account the fact that, over the past seven or eight years or so, well over 400 Cookie Patrol visits like this one have been made, thanks to the devoted service of our fine team of cookie bakers and patrollers.

That said, let me quickly make it clear that I'm not suggesting that people are drawn to Saint Paul's just because we give them a Bible and some cookies. What I do believe is that they see here what they're looking for in a church: gifted, competent leaders intent upon proclaiming Jesus Christ; also vibrant educational, youth, and music ministries; opportunities that are available to anyone who wants to serve God and others; and an inviting and welcoming congregation where fellowship abounds.

And the cookies help, too.

EDWARD KIMBLE

What do the apostle Andrew and Edward Kimble have in common? I suspect that you are all more familiar with the apostle than you are with anyone named Edward Kimble; but the truth is that both made their mark as first-rate recruiters for Jesus. It was Andrew, of course, who was one of the first called by Jesus and who then brought his brother, Simon, to Jesus. And, of course, Simon (Peter) it was whose sermon at Pentecost won some 3,000 converts to Christianity. And so the early church was born.

In his book Twelve Ordinary Men John MacArthur portrays Andrew as one who is very much unlike his bold and impulsive brother. Andrew's witness was mainly of the one-on-one type of encounter or, as MacArthur puts it, "doing what he loved best:- introducing individuals to the Lord .... laboring faithfully but inconspicuously."

But who is this Edward Kimble guy; and how might he possibly be compared to one of Christ's beloved followers?

Well, Mr. Kimble happens to have been a Sunday school teacher who led to Christ a young acquaintance of his. The story goes like this:

It was July 1, 1885 when Edward Kimble felt the tugging of the Spirit to share his faith with a young shoe salesman he knew. At first Kimble vacillated, unsure of how to continue. But he finally mustered his courage and entered the shoe store where he found the young salesman in the back room stocking shoes. The young man listened as Kimble boldly shared his faith story, then prayed, and received Jesus Christ that same day. His name was Dwight L. Moody; and he went on to become the greatest evangelist of his generation.

But the story doesn't end there. Several years later a pastor and well-known author by the name of Frederick B. Meyer heard Moody preach. Meyer was so deeply stirred by Moody's message that he himself embarked on a far-reaching evangelistic ministry.

Once, when Meyer was preaching, a college student named Wilbur Chapman accepted Christ as a result of his presentation of the gospel. Chapman later employed a baseball player to help him prepare to conduct an evangelistic crusade. That ballplayer, who later became a powerful evangelist himself, was Billy Sunday.

In 1924 a group of businessmen invited Sunday to hold an evangelistic campaign in Charlotte, North Carolina, which resulted in many people coming to Christ. Out of that revival meeting a group of men formed a men's prayer group to pray for the world. They prayed for Charlotte to have another great revival to which God sent yet another evangelist named Mordecai Hamm. Hamm went to Charlotte in 1934 to hold a crusade. On one of the last nights under the big tent, a tall, lanky young man walked up the aisle to receive Christ. That man's name was Billy Graham.

Talk about a chain of events! It all started with an ordinary Christian named Edward Kimble, who reached D.L. Moody, who reached Wilbur Chapman, who reached Billy Sunday, who reached Mordecai Hamm, who reached Billy Graham. Look at what God has done over these many years because of the faithfulness of one person.

Dare we be so bold as to think we, ordinary people ourselves, might be capable of doing what these men did? Can't the Holy Spirit work through us just as it did with these gentlemen?

Note: This story was found on the internet: Edward Kimble and the Shoe Salesman.

THE IMPACT OF PENTECOST

Question! If you were asked what event most dramatically changed your life, how would you respond? Might it be the day you met your spouse-to-be? Or the day you were married? Some might suggest that things really changed when they graduated from college. There could be a myriad of responses.

But I wonder how many would reply that the event which really shaped their life was their baptism. Many of us may not even know when our baptism took place, and I dare say that even fewer of us really understood until later in life what actually happened when we were baptized. But now, as Christians, we know and believe that, when we are baptized by water and the Word, we are reborn as children of God and received as members of the Church, the body of Christ. How great is that?

Now, what would your answer be if the question I just posed was altered slightly? "Which event in all of history had the greatest impact on you personally? I have to believe your reply might be quite different. When I put this question to my wife, she replied almost immediately, "Jesus' crucifixion." And who can argue with that? "After all," she continued, "when God offered us His only son to die on the cross for our sins, He showed us just how much He loves us." "True enough." I said, "But what about His resurrection? Many might contend that the events of Easter morning reshaped our lives for all eternity."

Where do you stand on this? Before you answer, let me toss in another historical event worthy of our consideration. Pentecost!

Think about it. This is a day marking the birth of the Christian church -- a day when we celebrate the descent of the Holy Spirit upon the apostles gathered in Jerusalem, empowering them to carry on Jesus' mission of service, healing, and love throughout the world. Without Pentecost, it might be said that the Apostles would not have been empowered to preach the Gospel, the Christian church might not have been born and, quite possibly, we would know little, if anything, about Jesus.

But, thanks to God, we do have Pentecost, and with the gift of the Holy Spirit at our baptism, our lives were remarkably shaped for a future of carrying forward the work begun by Jesus' apostles.

INTENTIONAL EVANGELISM

L ong before Billy Graham launched the first of his evangelism crusades some sixty plus years ago, yet another evangelist was preaching the Gospel to an estimated 100 million people around the world. I'm referring to Billy Sunday, a man who was described as the greatest evangelist since John the Baptist.

While preaching to a group in Richmond, Indiana back in 1922, Mr. Sunday spoke of a beautiful young, seventeen-year-old girl who had just died "with the dew of youth on her brow." (He had a wonderful way with words.)

As her casket was being borne from the church to the graveyard, a woman who had been her Sunday school teacher wept bitterly. Noticing her grief, the minister who had conducted the service asked the woman if the girl had been a Christian. The Sunday school teacher replied that she had noticed the girl growing careless with her companions and going into questionable places, and she said to the minister, "I was sure that you would speak to her, for you know more about these things." To which the minister replied, "No, I didn't speak to her. I intended to ... but, I didn't." He added, "I was sure that you would, because she was a girl, and you better understand one another." Both then decided to go see the girl's mother who said, "Yes, I noticed it. I used to plead with her, but she would get mad at me for interfering with her company. I hope that you spoke to her."

Neither of them had and, as Billy Sunday put it, the girl had gone to the judgment bar to witness against the three of them, for they had said nothing.

In his sermon, Mr.Sunday referred to this as the sin of indifference – the sin of neglect.

Coincidentally, I read this sermon of Mr. Sunday's at about the same time that we elected to call Pastor Stoner to lead our Mt. Laurel Initiative ministry, and I thought: What a shame it would be if we, as a congregation or as individuals, were to be indifferent to this outreach ministry to our neighbors in Mt. Laurel. What a shame it would be if we left this to someone else to attend to as the Sunday school teacher, the minister and the mother did in Mr. Sunday's sermon.

So, the question gets to be, "How can we help?"

Again, at the risk of sounding pious, we might begin by asking – by asking God if there is some way that we can help – by telling him that we don't want to be indifferent to this Mt. Laurel ministry. I'm only guessing, but God might suggest that we go and ask his agent, Pastor Stoner.

I like the word that Pastor Jost uses when he speaks of evangelism. He says we need to be intentional. We need to make it our intention to tell Pastor Stoner, "Here I am. Let me know how I can help."

Jesus tells us in his Great Commission to go and make disciples. Here we have a golden opportunity to do exactly what it is that Jesus wants us to do.

JOB INSTRUCTOR TRAINING

The training of our troops at the outset of World War II must have been a tremendous undertaking. The thought of transforming thousands of our young men and women -- many still in their teens -- into a combat-ready armed force in a matter of weeks! It staggers the imagination.

To accomplish this monumental task our military leaders developed and employed a training technique called JIT -- Job Instructor Training -- a simple yet effective training concept that embraced four steps: (1) Tell them; (2) Show them; (3) Let them do it; and (4) Follow up.

When reporting for active duty, every recruit received a certain amount of government issue -

- fatigues, boots, helmet, bedding, etc. For infantrymen, this issue included a rifle which they had to be trained to use; i.e., told and shown how to take it apart, clean it, reassemble it, and fire it. They were then taken to the firing range where they could actually do it. Before they could qualify as marksmen they were given follow up instruction to correct any mistakes they had made. Eventually they went on bivouac, where they honed their skills under fire until they were combat-ready.

It might be a little bit of a stretch, but when you think about it, as Christians, we are trained in much the same way, aren't we? God teaches us -- ordinary men and women just like those young recruits -- and He transforms us into "combat-ready" disciples -- the only difference being that the military relied on combat-experienced trainers using tried and true training manuals, while we look to our Sunday school teachers, pastors, and worship leaders with "training manuals" of their own -- especially prepared lesson plans, as well as Luther's Small Catechism, and the Holy Bible. As we complete our training, God assigns us a mission just as our G.I.s received theirs.

In her book A Story Worth Telling, Pastor Kelly Fryer writes of God's "Central Mission" for us -- Evangelism -- telling the story of Jesus.

The way I see it, the most essential of the four step training process is the doing it. What we need is a kind of spiritual bivouac of our own where we can practice what we have learned. I believe we need to practice our skills under simulated conditions, just as our G.I.s did. After all, practice is what enables one to excel at almost anything, be it playing the piano, baking a cake, playing golf, whatever.

Pastor Fryer says, "God uses the church to provide the training needed to be effective at telling the story of Jesus in the world." And she underscores this need to practice telling it in the church first so that we can then confidently tell it to those outside the church walls who still don't know Jesus and what he has done for all of us.

GOING THE EXTRA MILE

You may recall the name: David Poling-Goldene. It was he about whom I wrote a couple of articles last year, drawing on his thoughts as to how Christians might witness for Christ in their daily lives. He offered us some ideas as to how we might share our faith - at home and also at work. I also promised to pass along to you some of his thoughts on witnessing in times of struggle and pain. Here's what Mr. Poling-Goldene has to say about that:

* Visit neighbors and friends when they are sick or hospitalized. Share a devotional booklet and offer a prayer.
* Deliver a meal or a plate of cookies to the family or person who is struggling with loss, tragedy or illness.
* Share a cassette tape of uplifting, encouraging Christian music. Or they may enjoy listening to a recording of one our worship services.
* Mow the lawn, shovel the driveway, buy groceries, or clean the house without waiting to be asked. Then share why you were motivated to care in such a way.
* Recognize the variety of issues that bring pain to people's lives (financial crisis or loss, death, illness, divorce, abuse, etc.) Be a listening ear. Share how God has carried you in moments of personal struggle.
* Send cards, more than once, with encouraging words of scripture.

As I reviewed his suggestions, it occurred to me that many of you may already be doing most of what he recommends. God Bless You!

IT'S ONLY A QUARTER

This month's story comes to us compliments of Don Rousseau, Outreach Challenge leader at Faith Lutheran, the church our daughter, Linda, and her family attend in North Palm Beach, Florida. Don found it on the internet and titles it: "It's only a Quarter."

Several years ago a preacher from out-of–state accepted a call to a church in Houston, Texas. Some weeks after he arrived, he had occasion to ride the bus from his home to the downtown area. When he sat down, he discovered that the driver had accidently given him a quarter too much in change. As he considered what to do, he thought to himself: 'You'd better give the quarter back. It would be wrong to keep it. Then he thought: 'Oh, forget it. It's only a quarter. Who would worry about this little amount?' Anyway, the bus company gets too much fare; they will never miss it. Accept it as a gift from God and keep quiet.'

When his stop came, he paused a moment at the door, and then he handed the quarter to the driver and said: 'Here, you gave me too much change.'

The driver, with a smile, replied 'Aren't you the new preacher in town? 'Yes, he replied.'

Well, I've been thinking a lot lately about going somewhere to worship. I just wanted to see what you would do if I gave you too much change. I'll see you at church on Sunday.'

When the preacher stepped off the bus, he literally grabbed the nearest light pole, held on, and cried 'Oh God, I almost sold your Son for a quarter.'

Our lives are the only Bible some people will ever read. This is a really scary example of how much people watch us as Christians, and will put us to the test. Always be on guard and remember; you carry the cross of Christ on your shoulders when you call yourself 'Christian.'

* Watch your thoughts; they become words.
* Watch your words; they become actions.
* Watch your actions; they become habits;
* Watch your habits; they become character.
* Watch your character; it becomes your destiny.

Don said he loved this story, and it made him think: How would I have reacted if I had been given more change than I was due? More importantly, how will I react the next time? And what about you? What if the mistake was worth thousands of dollars? Would this make a difference?

Jesus answered, "I am the way and the truth and the life. No one comes to the Father except through me." John 14:6 (NIV) You and I, like that pastor in the story, are Christ's ambassadors. We're his disciples. We are His example in our words and in our whole life no matter where we are, what we are doing, or who we are with. We should always be aware, even on guard, as to how we relate to others. We never know when or who will be looking at us to see if we truly believe that Jesus is real.

For we are God's workmanship, created in Christ Jesus to do good works, which God prepared in advance for us to do. Ephesians 2:10 (NIV)

Thanks for sharing this with us, Don.

A LIFETIME GUARANTEE

In Paul's letter to the Romans, he pleads with them to give their bodies as a "living and holy sacrifice to Christ for all that He has done for them.(12:1) How are they to respond to this? And how are we to respond? Do we take this literally as a command to sacrifice our bodies as Christ did for us on the cross?

Thankfully, Paul clarifies this for us as we read further. He says we should "let God transform us into a new person by changing the way we think." When we do this, Paul says we will learn to know God's will for us."(v.2)

But, what about that word "transform?"

Here again, Paul seems to understand our need for direction. He writes of the "different gifts for doing things well" - - prophesy, serving, encouraging, leadership, showing kindness, loving, honor, hospitality, and much more.

I believe the key is in the Identifying of our gifts. The Holy Spirit can help us with this if we ask him, and He can show us how to use our gifts to build his family, i.e.; make disciples and grow Christ's church. But we need to work together.

In his teaching, Paul uses the concept of the human body to teach Christians how to do this – how to live and work together. For this to happen, we have to remember that God wants to be our friend, which is only going to happen when we remain close to him -- when we invite him into our hearts.

Let's remember that Paul had been transformed by Jesus on the road to Damascus. He had been a persecutor of Christians and was transformed into a preacher for Christ. God had big plans for Paul, as he does for us, also.

Have you ever been transformed? I know that many of you have, and I believe that I have, too, or at least, I am a work in progress. In my case, I believe God has found someone in need of a complete overhaul; or, at least a major tune-up. And, it has taken a long time -- years, in fact. But, God has given me time; and I thank and praise him for that. And, what a joyful experience it has been.

What I'm getting at is that some of us may have to be patient. Our transformation may not be as immediate as Paul's was. I don't know about you, but I'm finding this transformation experience to be a joyful one- – so much so that I would not hesitate to recommend God to any of you who feel a need for being transformed. He does good work, and He offers a life-time guarantee – in fact, an eternal guarantee. And it's cost-free – paid for in full by Jesus on the cross.

NEW COVENANT MINISTRIES

Most of you have heard or read Jesus' Greatest Commandment any number of times, and some, I'm sure, can recite it from memory: "You shall love your God with all your heart, and with all your soul, and with all your mind.... And the second is like it: You shall love your neighbor as yourself." (Matthew 22:38)

You may have noticed that Jesus said you "shall" love your God ...." He didn't say that you should love, or that he would like it if you did. He specifically said that you shall love him. It's a command, isn't it?

Many of you, like me, served in the military and remember that there were certain things that we were commanded to do – like – report for basic training or boot camp; or to go overseas, or to police the area, or report for KP duty. And we followed these orders. We didn't say "Oh, do I have to?" or "Why do I have to go?" We were expected to be obedient to our superiors - no ifs, ands, or buts, about it! If we weren't, there were dire consequences.

Why is it, then, that we find it so hard to obey the commands issued from our heavenly Father, or Jesus, our Lord of Lords - or that we so easily take the name of our Lord in vain, or worship other gods, like wealth and material goods?

And what about his Greatest Commandment? For me, the first part isn't so hard. I may not always show it, but I do love my God. When I stop to consider everything that He has done for me, how can I not love him? It's that second part that I struggle with – the neighbor part. Just who is our neighbor? Have you ever tried to figure that out?

I have an idea that Jesus would tell us that it's the poor and the sick, the hungry and the needy. Aren't they the people he went to? Richard Stearns maintains in his book, The Hole in Our Gospel, that these are the people who represent the "hole"- the people whom most of the world treats with indifference. He believes that the few who do respond to their needs are those who do it in tangible ways to show their love for their neighbor – those whose lives are characterized by acts of love.

One such group was recently brought to my attention. You may have heard of New Covenant Ministries in nearby Camden, New Jersey. It's a gathering of volunteers who are reaching out to help those living in this, neighboring, poverty-stricken city –committed people who have found tangible ways to show their love for their neighbors through a variety of ministries – a Street ministry, a Nursing Home ministry, a Prison ministry, a Housing ministry, a Food Bank ministry, a Prayer ministry, a Bicycle ministry, and many others. In one year alone some 800 bicycles were given to children whose parents lacked the money to buy their child a bike, a gift that most of our children take for granted. These are bicycles that are collected, repaired, cleaned, and maintained by volunteers throughout the year.

But it's not just bicycles that are donated. Add to that, toys, hats, gloves, and other gifts that are offered – all loving reminders that Jesus loves the little children.

It was last Christmas that I first heard of New Covenant Ministries and the awesome ways other Christians are reaching out in love to our neighbors in Camden. My son, John, recently shared with me an e-mail that he received from a fellow member of his church describing the people who, indeed, are bent on making disciples by doing something for those in need – and doing it here and now. These people are disciples themselves who are from all church backgrounds; make you feel as if you have belonged to this ministry forever; welcome you with open arms and the love we share with Jesus;

who come together with a common goal of loving others, feeding them, clothing them and, above all – telling them about Jesus;

who believe their ministry is all about Jesus and has absolutely nothing to do with them.

OPRAH -- ROLE MODEL AND DIFFERENCE MAKER

Oprah! Oprah! Oprah! What's the big deal? It's only another daytime female talk show.

Why is everybody getting all worked up just because her show is going off the air?

When I turned on the six o'clock news on the final day of her show, I found out why. What an eye-opener that was for me! Could I have been wrong about Oprah? Nah!

But the more I watched, the more I became convinced that I was wrong. (That's twice this year.) But truly, this is a remarkable woman—a real difference-maker. Should I "google" her to find out more? Good idea!

I found out just how much of a difference she has made over the past twenty-five years – not just for her viewers, but for people around the world. What a loving and grateful audience she had! Beautiful messages of gratitude and affection from everyone, everywhere. I like this one which I found very tender.

"God has used you to touch the hearts and souls of so many! I have been struggling with finding my purpose for years, and then I found it just days before the airing of your last show. I also believe that God gives people special gifts that help them achieve their purpose, and you have used your gifts in a most uplifting way. I thank God for the teachings he has bestowed upon me through you. Please know that you have truly been a blessing to me!"

Similar accolades have poured in from fans around the world. And what dreams she has brought to fruition for others!

Oprah's Angel Network founded on the simple idea that we all have the power to make a difference. And so she did, awarding six million dollars in grants to U.S. charter school programs;

The Oprah Winfrey Leadership Academy for Girls which she established to give back some of what she had been given;

Sixty schools built in undeveloped countries around the world.

Twenty-five years (4,561 episodes) of history-making, life-changing, spiritually-uplifting television – the highest-rated talk show in American history.

Actually, she considered quitting after twelve years but she realized: "I had no right to quit coming back from a history of people who had no voice, who had no power; and I have been given this blessed opportunity to speak to people, to influence them in ways that can make a difference in their lives…." Oprah's current slogan: Live Your Best Life! And she seems to be doing just that.

Stay tuned! She has her OWN network now.

So, there you have it, ladies. Your own role model, par excellence! But, what about us gentlemen? Who do we have to look up to? World leaders who can't find a way to live together in peace? Steroid cheating athletes?

Actually, if we give it a little thought, we will find that there is hope for us. All we need to do is page through our Bibles and we'll find many world-class role models. How about our Gospel writers and what they have to tell us? And let's not overlook others like Paul and Peter, David and Solomon; and, of course, Jesus, the king of all role models. All of them give us words of hope and promise that we can share with others.

"For God so loved the world that he gave his only Son, so

that everyone who believes in him may not perish but may have eternal life." (John 3:16)

"We know that all things work together for good for those who love God, who are called according to his purpose." (Romans 8-28)

"Therefore I tell you, do not worry about your life, what you will eat or what you will drink, or about your body, what you will wear….."(Matthew 6:25-33)

"Do not let your hearts be troubled. Believe in God, believe also in me. In my Father's house there are many dwelling places. If it were not so, would I have told you that I go to prepare a place for you? And if I go and prepare a place for you, I will come again and take you to myself, so that where I am, there you may be also." (John 14:1-3)

"See what love the Father has given us that we should be called children of God; and that is what we are….." (1 John 3:1)

"If you abide in me, and my words abide in you, ask for whatever you wish, and it will be done for you." (John 15:7) But, aren't we told elsewhere in Scripture that our Lord knows what we need? Perhaps that is what we should be asking for – not for that which we desire. What do you think?

Of course, this doesn't even scratch the surface of what it means to be a child of God, loved as only he knows how. But I did feel that these are words of hope and promise that we can treasure in our hearts.

A SIMPLE ACT OF KINDNESS

This story was emailed to me by my nephew, Tim Jonathan. It is titled Inmate Football, and I believe it tells a story of kindness unlike any you have heard before.

There was an unusual high school football game played in Grapevine, Texas. The game was between Grapevine Faith Academy and the Grapevine State School. Faith is a Christian school, and Gainesville State School is located within a maximum security correction facility.

Gainesville State School has 14 players. They play every game on the road. Their record is 0-8, and they've only scored twice. Their fourteen players are teenagers who have been convicted of crimes ranging from drugs to assault to robbery. Most had families who had disowned them. They wore out-dated, used shoulder pads and helmets. Faith Academy was 7-2. They had 70 players, 11 coaches, and the latest equipment.

Chris Hogan, the head coach at Faith Academy, knew the Gainesville team would have no fans and it would be no contest, so he thought: "what if half of our fans and half of our cheerleaders, for one night only, cheered for the other team?" He sent out an email to the faithful asking them to do just that. "Here's the message I want you to send," Hogan wrote. "You're just as valuable as any other person on the planet."

Some folks thought he was nuts. One player said, "Coach, why are you doing this?"

Hogan said, "Imagine you don't have a home life, no one to love you, no one pulling for you. Imagine that everyone had pretty

90

much given up on you. Now, imagine what it would feel like and mean to you for hundreds of people to suddenly believe in you."

The idea took root. On the night of the game, imagine the surprise of those fourteen players when they took the field, and there was a banner the cheerleaders had made for them to crash through. The visitor stands were full. The cheerleaders were leading cheers for them. The fans were calling them by their names. Isaiah, the quarterback-middle linebacker said, "I never in my life thought I would hear parents cheering to tackle and hit their kid. Most of the time, when we come out, people are afraid of us." You can see it in their eyes, but these people are yelling for us. They knew our names."

Faith won the game, and after the game, the teams gathered at the fifty-yard line to pray. That's when Isaiah, the teenage convict-quarterback surprised everybody, and asked to pray. He prayed, "Lord, I don't know what just happened, so I don't know how or who to say thank you to. But I never thought there were so many people in the world who cared about us,"

On the way back to the bus, under guard, each one of the players was handed a burger, fries, a coke, candy, a Bible, and an encouraging letter from the players from Faith Academy.

What an incredible act of Christian witness and kindness that was. Proverbs 11:17 says, "your own soul is nourished when you are kind." Proverbs 3:27: "Do not withhold good when it is in your power to act."

Be kind to someone this week. You might be amazed at what God will do with a simple act of kindness.

OUR WITNESSING DNA

Have Lutherans lost their witnessing DNA?

It was with this question that Pastor Barry Benson (Shepherd of the Hills Lutheran Church, Sparta, N.J.) opened his Telling the Story workshop that I recently attended. In his own way, I believe the good pastor was reminding us that proclaiming the gospel has never been considered something at which we Lutherans have excelled. This touches a nerve with me because, I have to confess that there have been times when I felt somewhat ill at ease about speaking to others of Jesus. This may be true of some of you as well. I have heard others say (and perhaps you have too) that we are just a little too laid back when it comes to speaking our faith. If this is true, what's the remedy? And does it really matter all that much?

Yes, I think it does matter. Jesus tells us, "Those who are ashamed of me and of my words, of them the Son of Man will be ashamed when he comes in his glory ...." (Luke 9:26).

How dreadful the thought of any of us being portrayed in such a way! Don't we all long to be on the very best of terms with our Lord, our Savior, our friend? Of course we do; and I believe that Pastor Benson's thoughts on this matter can be helpful to us.

He maintains that we could witness more effectively if we did a better job of listening.

He contends that witnessing begins with the other person. It's not about us. To this, I believe Pastor Jost might add that we should be "intentional" about listening.

If we first listen with concern, we might then find that our faith story will come more easily.

The Holy Spirit will tell us when to speak and how.

Jesus says this very thing in Matthew 10:19-20: "….Do not worry about how you are to speak, or what you are to say; for what you are to say will be given to you at the time; for it is not you who speak but the Spirit of your Father speaking through you."

At the right time, he might simply suggest we invite this other person to "come and see."

A WHAT IF SITUATION

While delivering a Thanksgiving Eve sermon, Pastor Jost once reflected upon Jesus' last encounter with the ten lepers he met while passing through Samaria on his way to Jerusalem. You remember the story from Luke 17 when the ten men cried out "Jesus, Master, have mercy on us." All ten were healed of their dread disease by Jesus; yet, only one of them thanked Him for what he had done. And that man was a Samaritan. Rather an astonishing story, given those relationships of the Jews and Samaritans had been contentious for some time.

Jesus asked about the other nine who were healed. "Has no one returned to give glory to the Lord except this foreigner?"

Jesus continued on his journey toward Jerusalem; but nothing more is said in Luke's account of where this Samaritan went. So, as I left the Sanctuary that Wednesday evening, I asked Pastor if there was any chance that the Samaritan who was healed might have caught up with the other nine – who were also healed – and said something like: 'Hey, look, Jesus has healed all of us. Let's hurry and tell others of this miracle he has done for us."

"That's an interesting question," Pastor said. "Why don't you write a story about it?" So, here goes!

Could this be one of those "what if" situations? What if all, or at least some, of these men had hurried home to show their family and friends how they had been cleansed? And by a Jew, no less. Something like what happened in John's Gospel story (fourth chapter), when the Samaritan woman met Jesus at Jacob's well; and Jesus said to her "I am the Messiah for whom you are waiting." Whereupon she ran back to the village from whence she had come and exhorted everyone to come and see.... So the people came streaming from the city.... And many believed.

But, for whatever reason, Luke makes no mention of such witness by these nine healed lepers. Perhaps God had other plans.

Now, please don't get me wrong. In no way am I suggesting that I could improve on Luke's writing. His story is what it is – the inspired word of God. (2 Timothy 3: 16-17) And there must be nothing added to it or taken away. It's just that I thought it would have been nice if this story of the lepers could have ended something like the story of the Samaritan woman at the well who rushed off to tell others to come and see the wonderful Messiah she had just met. Oh, that we all might have such a close encounter with our Lord Jesus!

Just imagine! What if these men who had been so miraculously healed by Jesus had, in fact, witnessed of their good fortune to their Samaritan families and friends? Once this good news had been made known throughout Samaria, might not there have followed more brotherly relations between the Jews and Samaritans?

Or are we left to believe that the tensions that existed then in that region remain with us today? I guess we'll never know.

EL HOMBRE

A s a boy growing up in the depression years of the 1930s, there weren't many days that I had a few pennies jingling in my pocket. But when I did, I made a bee line for Mr. Carlson's Drug Store to buy a pack or two of bubble gum – not so much for the gum as for the baseball cards inside. Like many of my pals, I had a really neat collection of stars like Joe DiMaggio, Bob Feller, and Luke Appling, to name a few. Whenever we obtained duplicates of players' cards, my friends and I enjoyed trading them for others we didn't have. But there was one guy whose card I never traded, and that was Stan Musial of the St. Louis Cardinals – better known as Stan the Man.

Baseball fans today are cheering the on-the- field performance of yet another surefire Hall of Famer. His name – Jose Alberto Pujols Alcantara – otherwise known as Albert Pujols, or El Hombre, which translates to the Man. I won't bore you with his "stats" or his numbers except to say that he has already received almost every award there is. What really sets this man apart, however, is his off-the-field performance.

Born in the poverty-stricken Dominican Republic and raised by his grandmother, Albert's childhood must have been much like ours during the depression – only much worse. While we would often fix a broken bat with a hammer and nail, he remembers playing catch with limes and wearing a glove made from a milk carton.

At age eighteen, Albert met and fell in love with a young woman named Dierdre. Dee Dee, as Albert called her, already had a baby girl who was born with Down syndrome. But that mattered little to Albert. He and Dee Dee fell in love, married, and honeymooned in Peoria, Illinois, home of a minor league affiliate of the St. Louis Cardinals, where Albert made his first stop on his way to the top.

Before long, Albert's life began to change dramatically, as Dee Dee began sharing with him the love of Jesus. "My most exciting moment came when I asked Jesus to come into my life," Albert confessed. "If it weren't for Jesus, my life would have no purpose." As he puts it, baseball is simply a platform to elevate Jesus Christ.

A few years ago, Albert and his wife founded the Pujols Family Foundation, a charity dedicated to the love, care, and development of people with Down syndrome and their families. Their Mission Statement: "Faith, Family, and Others." Albert believes his faith is central in his life and offers Ephesians 2:8-9 as his reason why. "For it is by grace you have been saved through faith, and this not of your own doing; it is a gift of God…" Good News for all of us!

Albert also draws our attention to the last word in their mission statement: "Others!" What they have in mind, of course, is Jesus' Great Commission to "Go and make disciples of all nations…" found in Matthew 28:19. Albert's response to this came in 2006 after the Cardinals won the World Series for the first time in twenty-four years. He said it wasn't their victory that was his personal favorite moment; it was seeing two of his friends and teammates come to know Jesus as their Lord and Savior.

My sources for this article: The March, 2009 issue of Sports Illustrated and www.puholsfamilyfoundation.org.

PETER'S MIRACLE

You may very well recall this story of Peter and John found in the third chapter of Acts. It's the story of their encounter with the man who was lame from birth and was placed each day outside the Temple gate where he could beg for alms from those entering for prayer services. (I believe the story is easier to tell if we give this man a name. Let's call him Harry.)

And so it goes that this crippled man, Harry, took notice of Peter and John entering the Temple and appealed to them for money. Peter replies that he has no silver or gold "but I give you what I have. In the name of Jesus Christ, the Nazarene, get up and walk." Taking Harry by the hand, Peter helped him up; and Harry's feet and ankles were "instantly healed and strengthened, and he began to walk." Not only was he walking, but he leaped for joy and praised God, and "he went into the Temple with them. (v. 18)

What a story! As it continues, I believe you will begin to observe some interesting side stories to this one of Peter's miracle. First, you will notice that Harry went into the Temple with Peter and John. (v.8) This raises a question in my mind: Was he invited in by Peter and John, or was it because he was always left outside the Temple that he was determined to go in on his own? I'd like to think that Harry was asked to join them – perhaps to give him an opportunity to offer a prayer of thanksgiving for his wondrous healing. After all, it was a prayer service.

Paul continues his tale: "All the people saw him walking and heard him praising God. When they realized it was the lame beggar they had seen so often ...., they were absolutely astounded. (v.v. 9-10)

This may suggest another side story: When the worshippers recovered from their astonishment, what did they do? I'd like to think they hurried to tell others to come and see for themselves of this awesome miracle. After all, this was sensational news.

And further in this story (v.v. 12-15) we might find yet another thought upon which to ponder. Peter sees all of these goings on as an opportunity to address the crowd. He wanted everyone to understand that it was God, not he, who "brought glory to his servant Jesus" by performing this miracle of healing – adding that this was the same Jesus whom they had rejected and killed .... "but God raised him from the dead. And we are witnesses of this fact!" How's that for telling it like it is?

A Bible teacher by the name of Warren Wiersbe offers some of his insight on this story, pointing out that it is a vivid illustration of salvation: "He was born lame, and all of us are born unable to walk so as to please God....The man was also poor, and we as sinners are bankrupt before God, unable to pay the tremendous debt that we owe Him (Luke 7:36-50).

With all due respect, Mr. Wiersbe, may I comment on your insights with a couple of my own?

We may have been born unable to please our heavenly Father; but, with his life and his teachings, Jesus tells us how our lives should be led so as to be in keeping with God's will. And we also have been gifted with the Holy Spirit to guide and counsel us as to how we should live God-pleasing lives. Secondly, we may have been born bankrupt; but there is no more debt. As believers, we know that Jesus paid our way in full on the Cross.

Somehow it was easy for me to relate to Harry's healing at the hands of Peter. A couple of years ago, I experienced some rather serious health issues of my own, albeit nothing on the scale of being unable to walk for a lifetime. Yet I feel certain that my recovery was something of a miracle also. There is no doubt in my mind that your prayers had a lot to do with this. Thanks to you and to God for his healing! Just as Peter was able to do for Harry, I am certain that God used the skilled hands of a neurosurgeon and his operating team to accomplish a miracle of healing for me.

EVIDENCE OF JESUS' DIVINITY

" **I** believe; help my unbelief!" (Mark 9:24 RSV) These are the words Jesus heard. from the father whose son was possessed of an evil spirit. He said to Jesus, "….If you are able to do anything, have pity on us and help us." That little word "if" reveals something of the father's uncertain faith, doesn't it? So he cries out for Jesus' help.

After all, it happened to Thomas, didn't it? He wanted evidence that Christ had risen.

Such was the case with a man by the name of Lee Strobel, an award-winning journalist and legal affairs editor for the Chicago Tribune.

Strobel was an atheist who wanted answers. So he spent almost two years questioning leading theologians around the world, investigating the Gospel and Christianity. When he finished, he was convinced that Jesus Christ is who he claims to be; and he accepted Jesus as his Lord and Savior.

What convinced him was the evidence he found – evidence of Jesus' miracles, his crucifixion, and his resurrection. He found writings about Jesus dating back almost to the time that Jesus lived. What really impressed Strobel was Paul's account (1 Corinthians 15: 3-7), which gives names of eyewitnesses to these magnificent events during the last years of Jesus' ministry.

Strobel adds that the single most powerful bit of evidence he found was the eyewitnesses who reported on Jesus' resurrection; concluding that they must have really believed what they were proclaiming. After all, they were willing to die rather than disavow their claim that Jesus was the Son of God. These disciples knew for a fact that Jesus had risen, because they touched him, they talked with him, and they ate with him – all of this after their Lord had died on the cross and had risen again.

Those who are fortunate to possess a strong, unshakable faith in the Gospel may not need all this evidence. They accept this truth on faith. But those who say "help my unbelief" may find some solace in Strobel's book, The Case for Christ.

Peter cautions us in his first letter to "always be ready to make your defense to anyone who demands from you an accounting of the hope that is in you; yet do it with gentleness and reverence." Strobel's book may will you to become "ready."

POSITIVE IMPACTS ON HUMANITY

A s we enter the twenty-first century, you might find it an interesting exercise to think back and try to identify who, in your mind, had the most positive impact on humanity during the last hundred years.

The operative word in the last sentence is "positive." With that in mind we can eliminate such demons as Adolph Hitler and Joseph Stalin and, most recently, Slobodan Milosevic, Saddam Hussein, and Osama ben Laden. So let's think positive.

Are there any whose names come to mind? Billy Graham might head my list – or possibly Mother Theresa. How about Mohandas Ghandi or Martin Luther King, or the man who entertained the world, Walt Disney – or perhaps Henry Ford or Jonas Salk? No doubt you can recall others whose lives have made for a better world.

One such person came to my mind a few weeks ago as I listened to one of Kathy Knodt's sermons. She was telling us about how the Bible is so full of beautiful stories that need to be told. This brought to mind the name of CORRIE ten BOOM, a spinster daughter of a Dutch watchmaker who was arrested by the Nazis for sheltering Jews during the occupation. But, more importantly, Corrie was a woman of remarkable faith. She and her sister, Betsie, shared their faith with hundreds of women interred with them at Ravensbruck, the notorious women's extermination camp in Germany. Their tale of life – and death (Betsie died while in prison) amid unspeakably brutal treatment at the hands or their Nazi captors is told in Corrie's book, The Hiding Place.

Corrie's most treasured possession while in prison was her

Bible; and with it she brought Jesus to hundreds of her fellow prisoners who hungered for the good news of salvation. Corrie ten Boom told the story during those long dark months of her imprisonment.

Their dream (Corrie's and Betsie's) and their prayer while in prison was that they might somehow be able to provide a home for any who survived Ravensbruck – a place where they could be loved and cared for.

While close to death, Betsie told her sister that we must tell the people what we have learned here. We must tell them that there is no pit so deep that He is not deeper still.

After her release and her return to Holland in 1945 Corrie came to realize that she had been spared so that she could speak of Jesus' love and salvation – and that God would provide the courage and the words. Remarkably, one of those who heard her speak was a wealthy, aristocratic lady who did, in fact, provide her with a home like that which she and Betsie had dreamed of.

And Corrie continued to tell her story for many years after the war. Hers was a story of handling separation from loved ones – facing death – loving your enemies – and forgiveness.

As I listened to Kathy's sermon about telling the story of Jesus, it occurred to me that Corrie ten Boom, while not as well-known as others we might name has, with her witness, truly had an enormous positive influence on the lives of hundreds and thousands of people around the world.

EVANGELISM FROM A DIFFERENT PERSPECTIVE

You may recall that last month we reflected on two topics: our neighbor, for one; and also evangelism. This month I would like to examine how I believe the two can work together.

Neighbor, first! Let's be honest! Most of us think of our neighbor as our next-door neighbor, or perhaps a nearby resident, or an acquaintance. Here at St. Paul's we reach out to our neighbors at Bridge of Peace Church in nearby Camden.

Richard Stearns (I'm going to mention his name often), President of World Vision, USA maintains that we should expand our vision and think of our neighbors on a global scale; especially our poverty-stricken neighbors in Uganda, Kenya, Sudan, and other African nations. Now more than ever before we are learning that these are neighbors where thousands upon thousands are dying every day from HIV/Aids, malaria, polio, tuberculosis, pneumonia, and thousands more are trying desperately to cope with other health issues, vitamin deficiencies, parasites, and other major tropical diseases often resulting from an urgent need of fresh water.

Mr. Stearns informs us that these horrendous conditions have existed for generations. We just didn't know about them or, if we did, we ignored them or looked the other way because they were "over there".

With the instant world-wide communications available to us via satellites, television, and the internet, we now are aware of what's happening over there. Not only that, Mr. Stearns insists we have access to them with intercontinental airways; and we have the ability to aid them through such institutions as the World Health Organization, Centers for Disease Control, and the National Institutes of Health.

Putting it another way, he asks how we would feel if we read in the newspaper of hundreds of children dying of malnutrition from famine in Africa. We would be saddened, of course; but eventually we would turn the page or change the channel and go on about our daily routines.

But Mr. Stearns then goes on and asks us to imagine how we might feel if we found one of these starving African children on our front doorstep as we left for church on a Sunday morning. "We'd most certainly respond with urgency" he says "and we would rush the child to an emergency room, offering to pay whatever the cost." All of a sudden this suffering child and the famine we had read about became intensely personal for us.

Quoting a report in Global Issues, Stearns tells us that, in one day alone, over 26,500 children around the world died of preventable causes related to their poverty; and he adds that it happened yesterday, and will happen again tomorrow, and the day after that. Almost ten million will be dead in the course of a year. "Even though we have the awareness, the access, and the ability to stop this," he asks "Why have we chosen not to? …. perhaps one reason being that they're not our kids who are dying. They are somebody else's.

I don't know about you; but this has given me a very different perspective of evangelism.

Until now I thought of evangelism as, first and foremost, telling others about Jesus, who he is, how he loves me, and what he has done for me and for everyone.

Please don't get me wrong. This is something I believe God wants from every one of us Christians. But somehow I have come to believe that we must first do something for those we are trying to reach, especially those whose circumstances are so terribly different from ours. We need to act lovingly toward them. Won't it become easier to tell others about our Savior if we first show them that we love them and want to help them? Let's let our light shine before others, so that they may see our good works and give glory to our Father in heaven (Matthew 5:16).

Citing Jesus' words in the Lord's Prayer, Stearns puts it very nicely .... "your will be done on earth as it is in heaven." He says that these words were and still are a clarion call that Jesus' followers are not just to proclaim the good news but to be the good news here and now.

Imagine! If we all did this, how we might change what seems to me to be a growing, less favorable image that many now seem to have of America as a world leader and Christianity, as a way of life.

Action springs not from thought, but from a readiness for responsibility.

Dietrich Bonhoeffer

HOW WE GLORIFY GOD

During one of his Bible Study sessions several years ago, Pastor Stoner remarked that the reason we are here on earth is to glorify God. At the time, I didn't ask him how that's done, but I wish I had. So, I'll ask it now. How *do* we glorify God?

When I told my wife, Laura, that I planned to address this issue in one of my articles, she thought a moment. Then she broke out in song with the very familiar:

Praise God from whom all blessings flow; Praise him all creatures here below; Praise him above ye heavenly host; Praise Father, Son, and Holy Ghost.

As Laura sang the Doxology, it brought to mind another praise-like melody that was popularized by Kay Kaizer and his orchestra way back in 1943, during the height of the second world war. It goes like this:

Praise the Lord and pass the ammunition; Praise the Lord and pass the ammunition;

Praise the Lord and pass the ammunition; And we'll all stay free.

The ammunition referred to by the lyricist was, no doubt, that which our troops needed to overcome our enemies in Europe, North Africa, the South Pacific, and Japan. In a manner of speaking, I can't help but think that our Lord has also given us quite an arsenal of spiritual "ammunition" to have at our disposal at such time as we might need it. Let's see what Scripture has to say about it.

* Matthew 22: 38 – Jesus' Great Commandment: "You must love the Lord, your God with all your heart, all your

soul, and all your mind. A second reminder is equally important: Love your neighbor as yourself."

* Matthew 28:19 – Jesus' Great Commission: "Therefore, go and make disciples ....teaching these new disciples to obey all of the commands I have given you."
* Matthew 10:32-34 - -"Everyone who acknowledges me publicly here on earth, I will also acknowledge in heaven.
* John 15:1-8 -- Jesus' teaching of the vineyard: He is the vine, and we are the branches; and we are to bear fruit for him. This, too, is how we glorify God.

Some other thoughts about this subject, perhaps not so scriptural, but food for thought:

* Tell others what Jesus has done for us – and for you, personally.
* Be like Jesus – or at least try to be.
* Work hard to serve the Lord and others. Use the time, the talents, and the treasures He has given us.
* Reach out to the poor and the outcasts. Pray for them.
* Thank God for his countless blessings.
* Be humble.
* Be hospitable.
* Encourage others – build up God's church.
* Honor the Sabbath – go to church.
* Do unto others as you would have them do unto you.
* Let your light so shine before others that they might see your good works and glorify your Father in heaven.

A PRODIGAL SON....RETRIEVED

Most of us are familiar with the biblical story of the prodigal son, who took his share of his father's inheritance and "squandered it in dissolute living." (Luke 15:13) And you may recall his older brother's bitter reaction to his father's joyous welcome upon the return of his youngest son.

For the longest time, whenever I heard this story, it seemed to me so very unfair that the older son received so little for all the years of loyal, obedient service he had rendered to his father. Why such a fuss over his kid brother just because he finally showed up after so many years of debauchery?

I simply didn't get it until, finally, it was explained to me that the father in the story represents our own ever-loving Father in heaven, who rejoices when one of his lost is found.

A story like this is beautifully told in a book I recently read, The Shield of Honor, written by George Morris. Like the biblical story familiar to many of us, this story to which I refer has it's beginning in London, where the protagonist leads a life of indulgence and indebtedness that gives rise to a prison term in the Tower of London. Upon his release, he finds forgiveness from his father, then sets sail aboard the Mayflower for the New World where he, too, begins a new life of repentance, and finds forgiveness and love with a fine young woman who leads him to Christ.

SEX-TRAFFICING SHELTER FILLED WITH SURVIVOR TALES....

The headline in a recent issue of the Burlington County Times. The article described quite graphically the horrible pain and deprivation three teenage girls suffered at the hands of sex predators across the country. It was only after three years of captivity that all three found shelter with Samaritan Women, a Baltimore, Maryland faith-based residential program - one of few in the nation dedicated to long-term help for the surging number of victims of human- trafficking. This is an issue of particular interest to Laura and me, as two of our granddaughters have taken this matter to heart.

You may recall a couple of articles I wrote a few years ago about the eldest of our four granddaughters, Dale, (age twenty-one), who spent six months training and working in Australia and Thailand with YWAM (Youth With a Mission). Their mission: to work with young Thai women, telling them about Jesus and teaching them work skills such as sewing and hair care, for example, so they would no longer have to rely on their bodies to make a living.

More recently, a second of our granddaughters, Robin Seitz, also age twenty-one, and now completing her final year at Auburn University in Alabama, has now committed her future to aiding victims of human- trafficking. Her hope is to intern next fall for a California organization - A21 Campaign – that is involved with human-trafficking on a global scale. Meanwhile, she is serving as president of a local non-profit organization – Friendship 21 - based in the Auburn community.

While recently discussing with Robin the remarkable work being done for sex-trafficking victims by Samaritan Women in the Baltimore community, and the difference this has made in their lives, I wondered aloud to her what might be done, if anything, for the predators. Are they to be left alone in their evil ways? Aren't they God's children, too? Think about it! If their lives can be turned around, transformed, if you will, wouldn't that bring an end to human- trafficking?

Let's pray for those scoundrels!

The next day I received an e-mail from Robin saying she agreed with me wholeheartedly. In fact, she had already made this a focus of her prayer ministry.

I have to wonder sometime how these youngsters already know so much about things it has taken me a lifetime to learn.

THE RAIN IN SPAIN

Many of you will recall the popular Broadway musical of the 1960's, My Fair Lady – the story of an arrogant, demanding Professor of Phonetics (Rex Harrison) who believes that the accent and tone of one's voice determines the person's prospects in society. So proud is Henry Higgins of his teaching skills that he boasts to an acquaintance, one Colonel Pickering that he could teach any woman to speak so "properly" that he could pass her off as a duchess at the Embassy Ball.

Well, as it happens, a young flower girl from the slums with a strong Cockney accent calls on the professor for speech lessons. Her name: Eiiza Doolittle (Audrey Hepburn). She says she wants to be a "lidy." Higgins, of course, welcomes her, but soon realizes that her thick accent is going to present quite a challenge.

After weeks of rigorous speech training, including one exercise of trying to speak with a mouthful of marbles, Higgins asks Eliza to pronounce the phrase "The Rain in Spain Stays Mainly in the Plain." She botches that, of course, and Higgins is about to give up on her. But suddenly, out of the blue, she slowly and properly pronounces the words. To which Higgins proclaims "She's got it – By George, I think she's got it." So proud is Higgins of his success with Eliza that he and Pickering both join her in a rousing rendition of "The Rain in Spain"

As Laura and I watched the rest of the film, it occurred to me that I had recently had such a "getting it" experience of my own. It wasn't so much that I didn't understand Jesus' command to "go and make disciples" as it was that, like Eliza, I didn't know how to do it.

Then, one day recently, as I was driving by our church, I took notice of the sign out front. The message was rather lengthy, but I was able to make out the first five words: "Faith is the first step." I thought: Could it be that I lacked enough faith to obey Jesus' command?"

When I reached home, I went directly to our bedroom and prayed "Please Lord, help me with this. Show me how to make disciples for you." Sure enough, soon afterward I remembered - or perhaps I read - that with God everything is possible (Matthew 19:26). Jesus' disciple, John, tells us pretty much the same thing (1 John 5:14-15), "And we are confident that he hears us whenever we ask for anything that pleases him." Well, I thought: certainly, it would please him if I made disciples for him. That's what he wants us to do. But I've got to remember that the first step is faith. I've got to trust him. When I think of all that he has done for me, why would I not want to trust him. That's a no-brainer.

You know, I think I could almost hear God shouting "Hallelujah! I think David has finally got it."

PROMISES FULFILLED

Many people, I believe, have certain habits or behavior patterns they follow until they become almost involuntary. I know that I do. For example, it has become my habit to evaluate things - almost anything - to assign a rating on a scale of one to ten, much like Olympic divers and gymnasts receive for their performances.

A crisp fall day, for example, with a clear blue sky and wispy clouds might receive a rating of 9.5 or 10. I have even been so bold as to assign a grade to our pastors' sermons - (like they really care what I think). Actually, there have been some sermons that were so good that I even awarded them an eleven. In years past it was my habit to evaluate my round of golf as we walked off the eighteenth green; but I don't do this anymore. It became too depressing.

You may think it strange, but I have done the same thing with my faith. Right now I would place it in the 8.0 to 9.0 range - pretty good, but not perfect. And that bothers me! Are you like that? Are there times when a shadow of doubt might be a little unsettling to your faith? There are times when I might even pray about this. A prayer book that I keep on the table next to my bed contains a prayer that begins: "Lord, I believe. Help Thou my unbelief. Strengthen Thou my weak and feeble faith..." This suggests to me there may also be others like me who believe their faith to be imperfect.

My dictionary defines faith as a confidence or trust in a person or thing; a belief that is not based on proof. Fortunately, for those of us who, like Thomas, feel the need of a little proof, we simply need to turn to scripture where we can arm ourselves with all kinds of proof.

Take, for example, the hundreds of Old Testament prophecies that have been fulfilled in the New Testament. I believe that it was shortly after his resurrection that Jesus reminded his disciples "everything written about me in the law of Moses, the prophets and the Psalms must be fulfilled." a few examples:

* Almost 700 years before Jesus' birth Isaiah tells us; "Look, the young woman is with child and shall bear a son, and shall name him Immanuel, which means "God is with us."(Isaiah7:14) Fulfillment of this virgin birth prophecy is found in Matthew 1: 22-23.

* Some 500 years before Jesus' birth his triumphal entry into Jerusalem is foretold in Zechariah 9:9: "Lo, your king comes to you, triumphant and victorious, humble and riding on a donkey, on a colt, the foal of a donkey." Again, Matthew provides fulfillment of this prophecy (Mt. 21: 4-5). John also relates this Palm Sunday story(John 12: 14-15).

* Here's another! (Psalm 22:1) "My God, my God, why have you forsaken me?" This same agonizing cry is found in Mark 15:34.

* The casting of lots for Jesus' clothes is described in Psalms 22:18 and, again, generations later, fulfilled in Mark 15:24, Mathew 27:35 and John 19:24.

All are solid evidence of Old Testament prophecies fulfilled by the Good News of Jesus Christ – absolute proof that Jesus is who he claims to be.

I am certain that there are many among you whose faith is strong enough that you do not require this kind of proof. But it's kind of nice, isn't it, to know that it's right there in the Bible, just in case.

SHE SAID 'YES'

Ann had just showered after a brisk hour of practice with her high school volleyball team. After toweling down and dressing, she noticed a picture of a pretty girl on the bench near her locker. The girl appeared to be about Ann's age. So she picked up the picture to see if it might be someone she recognized. Printed on the upper right corner was the girl's name: Cassie Bernall. And just below, in large print, were the words: She said YES – A Story of Hope from Columbine High.

It was then that Ann identified Cassie with the tragic shootings in Colorado some years back. Ann was only eleven at the time, but she vaguely remembered there had been several school- related shootings. She wondered: Could anything like that happen at my school? Opening the leaflet, Ann found printed the story of the shooting as the writer believed Cassie might have told it, if she had not been killed.

Now you, too, may recall Cassie as the courageous teenage girl who said, "Yes" to the boy holding a gun to her head and asking, "Do you believe in God?" Boldly answering" Yes," in a clear voice, Cassie lost her life on earth.

What you may not know is that, in the story as Cassie may have told it, she had recently made some bad choices of friends and other pursuits. When her parents learned of this, they grounded her from her old friends, transferred her to another school, and insisted she go to church and youth group.

Cassie felt this had changed her life. She learned of God's love and that Jesus died for her sins, and that, with her bold answer to the boy's demand, God had taken her into His loving arms in heaven.

By the time she had finished reading, Ann was crying.

Her friend, Barbara, had just entered the locker room and quickly asked, "What's the matter?" Ann handed her the leaflet, and Barbara read. Almost immediately, Barbara replied,

"Oh, Annie, this is just one of those tracts people take from door-to-door. My Mom says they're just a lot of baloney. Throw it away!" But Ann asked for it back and put it into her back pack.

While on the school bus heading home, Ann realized that she, too, had made some wrong choices. It had only been yesterday that, while having lunch with two other girls, she willingly allowed herself to be drawn into a conversation besmirching Emily Parker, one of their classmates. Emily was a tall, skinny girl, who had a hard time finding friends. At one point, Ann had even described her as "such a geek."

As the three girls got up with their trays, Ann noticed, to her chagrin, that Emily was seated alone at a nearby table and, most certainly, must have heard what had been said.

After dinner, Ann told her parents she had some homework and would be in her bedroom.

She went right to her back pack, retrieved the leaflet and reread Cassie's story. It was then that she noticed, for the first time, what was printed on the back: "Jesus is knocking at the door of your heart. (Rev. 3:20) Will you say yes and ask Him into your heart?"

Ann was so moved that she fell to her knees, beside her bed, and prayed, "Lord, I know that I am a sinner and need your forgiveness. I do believe that Jesus Christ died on the cross for my sins and rose again. I do want to surrender my life to you, Lord. Please, come into my heart and into my life. Amen."

Instantly, Ann knew that her prayer was answered. She

was forgiven. But what about Emily? Could Emily forgive her? Quickly she searched for Emily's phone number. When Emily answered, Ann blurted out, "Emily, I know that you heard my nasty remark about you in the cafeteria today - and I am so sorry. Can you possibly forgive me? I'd like to be your friend."

In her excitement, Ann hung up, not hearing Emily's reply, "That would be nice."

Realizing how bewildered Emily must be, Ann quickly redialed, and Emily answered after one ring. "Hi Em, it's me again. I was wondering. Tomorrow's Saturday. Would you like to have a sleepover tomorrow night? My parents just gave me the new DVD, Sisterhood of the Traveling Pants 2, for Christmas. Or, if you want, we could play Guitar Hero on our Wii. Then after church on Sunday, my mom could drive us to the mall, and we could hang out for a while and do a little shopping.

DON'T LET YOUR HEART BE TROUBLED

G ood health is not something to be taken for granted, is it? It's one of God's most precious gifts, something we need to take good care of. And it's free.

My dermatologist recently expressed some concern over a pre cancer condition on my forehead and suggested that, to be on the safe side, a biopsy should be taken to determine whether further treatment might be necessary. A week or so later, the doctor's technician called to say the biopsy was negative.

No cancer! I thanked her and hung up, thinking little more about it. Later, when I told Laura, she said, "Well, that's good news." Only then did I realize how fortunate I was. It was good news.

But we all know there will come a time when the news won't be so good. It could be a health issue, a son or daughter whose marriage is breaking up, a job loss, or even the loss of a loved one. What can we do at times like these? Prayer, of course, is one answer. This can be comforting to the afflicted. But is it enough? Might there be something we can do to help ease the hurt?

During one of his Bible studies, Pastor Stoner remarked that, when we learn of some person's bad fortune, why not simply ask if there something we can do to help. He added, "What's happening when we show our concern for someone like this? Aren't we saying to our friend that we really care for him/her – that we would like to listen?" When we listen, we may become aware of an opportunity to respond to this person's need in a meaningful way. You may recall something you heard in a Bible study or something you read in scripture that would speak to your friend's need.

Let's consider what might be the very worst news one might receive – the news that nothing more can be done to restore the health of a loved one. Is there anything of comfort one might say to such a person? I believe there is, and it's something we hear in almost every funeral service we attend: "Don't let your hearts be troubled. Trust in God, and trust also in me. There is more than enough room in my Father's home. If it were not so, would I have told you that I go to prepare a place for you? When everything is ready, I will come and get you, so that you will always be with me where I am." (John 14: 1- 3)

Think about it! What better news can you give someone than that our Savior has taken your loved one to live with him forever in heaven? Good new, indeed!

GOD'S GIFTS

I n addition to the cookies that are given to first time visitors, our welcome bag also includes a bright orange scriptographic booklet that is published by the Channing Bete Company. It's titled Be an Active Church Member."

Now I think we would be pretty hard-pressed to find another church whose members are more active than many of you are here at St. Paul's; so I'm going to resist the temptation to suggest that this booklet is intended mostly for those who are not actively involved in our church life. There's something here for all of us.

Remember: God has gifted us all in different ways. Let's pray about this. Let's ask the Lord to help us identify our gifts. And I'll bet that one of our pastors can tell you how you might put them to good use. Peter reminds us in his first letter (chapter 4:10) "....serve one another with whatever gift you have received."

THE ETHIOPIAN EUNUCH AND PHILIP

The Augsburg Press publication, Christ in Our Home, can be very helpful toward understanding Scripture. I found this to be true as I read the devotion for May 1st describing the captivating story of the apostle, Philip, and how he changed forever the life of the Ethiopian eunuch. I decided to feature this nice story in this month's issue of Chimes.

Imagine my surprise when, on Mothers' Day, May 10th, Pastor Stoner preached on this very same encounter that Philip had with the Ethiopian. Not so surprising, of course, was how expertly pastor related to us this beautiful outreach story. So, where does that leave me? What might I say that could possibly add to the understanding of this Scripture passage? Oh, well, I'm going to give it a shot anyway.

What I found noteworthy about this story was that an angel of the Lord first needed to direct Philip south to a desert road leading to Gaza where he might overtake the eunuch. It is here that the Holy Spirit takes over and points Philip toward the eunuch's carriage where he finds him reading from the book of Isaiah.

"Do you understand what you are reading?" Philip asks. "How can I," is the reply "unless someone instructs me?" Philip is then invited into the carriage and promptly seizes upon the opportunity to tell his new friend all about Jesus. And the eunuch listens. So inspired is he that he asks the apostle to baptize him. The story then closes as the two men take leave of one another – the eunuch continuing south to Ethiopia and Philip returning north to Caesarea.

But think about what Philip has accomplished here. For

all intents and purposes he has placed this new Christian in a position in a foreign land where he may well have won many more souls for God's kingdom. Yet, none of this would have happened were it not for the direction of our Lord Jesus and the words and counsel of the Holy Spirit.

Is it possible that we could be so empowered by Jesus and the Spirit that we could bear fruit as Philip did? Jesus tells us in John 14:13 that all we need do is ask in his name and we will be able to do anything.

Pastor Jost's 9:45 am study class between services on Sunday mornings has also underscored for those attending how Scripture can be understood more clearly as we study the Book of Faith and its Lutheran insights for Bible study. As Lutherans, we try to identify ourselves as the good soil of which Jesus speaks in Matthew 13:23: "those who truly hear and understand God's word and produce a harvest ..." This, of course, happens as we listen in worship and confer with one another in Bible study.

I would like to suggest one additional resource of which you may be aware that will increase our understanding of Scripture – that being a commentary written by a Christian theologian. If you don't already have a commentary, you should be able to find one in any nearby Christian bookstore. Matthew Henry's thoughts on this Philip/Ethiopian eunuch story are so recorded in his Concise Commentary: "Philip was directed to go to a desert. Sometimes God opens a door of opportunity to his ministers in very unlikely places ... The Ethiopian eunuch was convinced by the teaching of the Holy Spirit ... He was made to understand the nature of the Messiah's kingdom and salvation ..."

That May 1st devotional study mentioned above closes with this prayer: "God ... send me a Philip, and then send me as a Philip to my neighbor. In Jesus' name. Amen. "Note: Christ in Our Home devotional booklets can be found in the church narthex.

GOD'S NOT DEAD - GET THE WORD OUT

It's past ten o'clock on Friday night. Laura, Andy, and I have just returned home after watching the recently-released movie, God's Not Dead. And I want to get the word out. Go see this movie!!

If you can, get together as a family, or call a friend. Call someone, and enjoy it together. You will never regret it. Take it from me, your self-appointed movie critic.

It's a story of a young college student, a devout Christian, who finds his faith challenged by a philosophy professor who orders his entire class to disavow God, in writing, or face a failing grade. I'll tell you no more, except to say that this young student accepts the challenge in a way which is powerful and uplifting.

I give the movie five stars.

THE FIRST CONCERN OF THE CHURCH

T his month let's give some thought to needs.

For twenty plus years before retiring I worked for a chemical company that believed that the safety of its employees was no less important than earning a profit. Its management recognized the need to provide a safe work environment for its employees.

One of my responsibilities was the administration of our plant safety program. Fortunately I was reporting to a Plant Manager who fully embraced the company's safety policy. He assigned me the task of developing a safety suggestion system that would involve employees in the identification of unsafe working conditions in the plant and offering suggestions as to how these conditions might be improved. His logic was good: who was better qualified to do this than the Chemical Operators and other plant employees who understood the plant processes?

The new suggestion system turned out to be a huge success and played a key role in establishing our plant as one of the safest corporate-wide. Our need for safety had been addressed; and it had the added advantage of involving all employees in the business of their own safety.

Just as our employees' safety was a major concern of our company, I believe that it can also be said that evangelizing should be a first concern of the church. Doesn't that mean that we should make it our business to reach out to others in need? But just what is it that they might need?

Jesus tells us in Matthew 6 that our heavenly Father already knows what we need. If he can satisfy the needs of the birds and the lilies of the field, certainly we don't have to worry about what we're going to eat or wear. What then? What else do people need? Let's try to answer that question.

What about love; God's grace; faith; prayer? How about fellowship; or a visit to a shut-in; encouragement; uplifting; or peace of mind? How about those without a church family; or those who want to know more about Jesus, or how they might have a closer relationship with him? Aren't these all things that are needful to those whose lives are void or empty? I'm certain that you could add many more such needs.

One final question! Just where does one go to get these needs satisfied? To the mall? – or perhaps E Bay? I don't think so. How about church or almost any other house of worship that proclaims Jesus Christ as our Lord and Savior?

STARTING A CONVERSATION

C ommercials, whether on TV or radio, drive me to distraction. They're too long, too loud, and too often. But I confess, one of them recently caught my attention – before I could find my remote. I believe it was a Wells Fargo ad suggesting that, when someone starts a conversation, good things usually happen. My thought: Maybe! Maybe not!

When you tell your spouse, "I love you," certainly, some good things can happen. I believe also, some good things happen when you start a conversation about church - perhaps an upcoming event like Vacation Bible School, or Easter. Not so, however, when we gossip about someone, or allow ourselves to be drawn into such a conversation. Not a good idea!

Such an opportunity presented itself to me during one of our Bible study sessions. As we were talking about outreach to unbelievers, I asked, "Why don't we ask other Lutheran churches in our community to join us in organizing an outreach rally of sorts?" Let's call it a "Come and See" rally, inviting everyone in our community to come and see what can happen when Christ is placed first in our lives.

Stay with me on this, please.

I'm thinking something on a grand scale. Oh, it doesn't have to be like a Billy Graham crusade; but something BIG – a gathering planned, organized, and presented by all the Lutheran churches in our community; e.g., the Southwest district of our ELCA, New Jersey Synod – a manageable group of some six to eight churches.

Our goal: "Go and make disciples...." just as our Lord Jesus requires of us in his Great Commission. (Matthew 28:19-20) Let's invite everyone, especially unbelievers, people who still don't know Jesus, but would like to, skeptics, the unchurched – everyone.

Can it work? Certainly! Granted! It would take a lot of time – months, perhaps a year or more. Detailed planning would be needed. Reasonable, attainable goals should be set. Other considerations would need to be dealt with such as, rally dates and site locations, costs, budgets, publicity, music, guest speakers, visual aids, Synod aid and approval, perhaps. And, much more, no doubt.

Perhaps some thought might be given to scheduling these rallies to coincide with the 500th anniversary of the birth of the Lutheran church. Think; October 31, 2017, the date Martin Luther posted his 95 Theses.

Let's be positive, and think boldly. Remember what Jesus once told his disciples…. "with God everything is possible." (Mt 19:26)

First, let's pray about it. We know that, when we pray in Jesus' name for something that is in keeping with God's will, it's going to happen. So, let's get started.

THE VIRTUOUS ONE

During The 1930's, Gladys Aylward was to the millions of Chinese whom she served, very much like what Paul, Barnabas, Silas, and others were to the Gentiles and Jews during their missionary journeys over two thousand years ago.

Miss Aylward's story is told in a book written by Alan Burgess in 1957 titled The Small Woman. After you have read this brief synopsis of her life of service, I believe that you will agree that, while this woman was very small of stature, she was huge in the life of service she lived for her Lord and the people of China whom she served.

Soon after completing her exhausting journey from England to the tiny, inland town of Yangchen, Gladys and her seventy-three year old missionary mentor, Jennie Lawson, set to work converting Mrs. Lawson's living quarters into an inn where travelers and their mules might find good food and warm beds for a night before continuing inland with their cargo of coal, raw cotton, pots, and iron goods.

In the evening, after their traveling guests had washed and dined, the two women offered free entertainment in the form of stories about a man named Jesus. Over time, some became Christians and retold the stories to other muleteers at stops along the caravan trails. Thus, many seeds were planted, and the Good News of Jesus was carried inland to other Chinese provinces.

The young English lass quickly mastered the language of the Chinese but, tragically, their ministry was interrupted when Mrs. Lawson suffered from a fall and died. Gladys was left alone to run the mission, and had only the aid of a Chinese Christian named Yang, who was their cook.

But God had big plans for Gladys. News of her fine work soon reached the ears of the Mandarin of Yangchen, who informed her of a government decree ending the practice of foot- binding among Chinese women. Gladys was designated as foot-inspector and assigned the duty of enforcing the decree. Being ever alert for opportunities to spread the Gospel, Gladys readily accepted her new position.

Next! A riot broke out in the Yangchen prison, and Gladys was deputized to quell the riot. When several rioters are soon killed, Gladys quickly selects two spokesmen from among the rioters who inform her of the appalling, crowded conditions in the prison, the lack of enough food, and, worst of all, too much idle time. So, Gladys arranged for looms to be brought in so they could weave cloth, earn money, and buy their own food.

The Mandarin, acting on the advice of Gladys, devised a plan whereby relatives and friends of the prisoners could post a bond guaranteeing their good behavior; and every one of them eventually was released on bond.

The townspeople so admired their new friend that they began addressing her as "Ai-weh- dey," which means "The Virtuous One." The Mandarin declared that he was so gratified with the accomplishments of Ai-weh-dey that he wished to make her faith his own.

In 1936 Gladys Aylward officially became a Chinese citizen. And then the war came.

In 1938 Japanese planes bombed Yangchen, killing many and sending survivors into the mountains. Gladys often found herself behind enemy lines. Taking careful notice of their dispositions, she passed information on to the armies of China, her adopted country. When the enemy learned of her activities, a Japanese handbill was printed offering $100 for the capture of the Mandarin and Ai-weh-deh, dead or alive.

Gathering some 100 of her dependent children, Gladys and her flock fled Yangchen, determined to reach a government orphanage at Sian. For twelve days, they walked, often spending nights unprotected on the mountainsides before reaching Sian and safety. There she spent several years preaching, while at the same time starting a Christian church in Sian, and later serving at a leper settlement in Szechuan, near the border of Tibet.

With her health permanently impaired from injuries suffered during the war, this virtuous woman returned to England in 1947 and continued preaching until her death in 1970.

EVERYTHING

One of my favorite hymns is # 661 in our red worship hymnal titled I Love to Tell the Story. It has a beautiful melody and a powerful message as well. As Christians, we are to tell others the story of Jesus and everything he has done for us. It puts me in mind of what Jesus tells his disciples in his Great Commission found in the last chapter of Matthew's Gospel wherein Jesus commands his disciples to go and make new disciples and to teach them also that they are to obey all the commands he has given them. We are among those new disciples, are we not?

Over time, I have asked others how we can best speak about Jesus. The answer I often get is that, as Christians, we do this by the way we live. Well, that may be. But how do we actually tell Jesus' story?

This puts me in mind of what the blind man said to the Pharisees when his sight was restored by Jesus. "One thing I know: that though I was blind, now I see." Plain and simple, that's what Jesus meant to him.

Now, perhaps, you will allow me to ask a couple of questions. First, what exactly should we say? Well, we all have at least one thing in common from Him: the Bible and the inspired Gospel stories of the life Jesus lived for us, a life of teaching us how to love according to His Great Commandments. As I think about this, what seems to me to be most compelling about his life is his teachings.

He has taught us how to love as he has loved. He has taught us how to pray; e.g., The Lord's Prayer. His was a life of teaching us how to forgive as he forgives. And he has taught us his Golden Rule to do unto others what we would have them do unto us.

There is more about his life you might value even more highly than his teaching: His grace and his mercy, for example, or perhaps his suffering, his death on the cross, his resurrection, and his gift of the Holy Spirit to comfort and counsel us. And let's not overlook his promise of eternal life with him in heaven. What else?

He has given us the Ten Commandments to guide and direct us. With his suffering, his death, and his victory over death, Jesus has washed away all of our sins and given us access to our Father in heaven. And he has gone ahead to prepare a place for us in his heavenly home.

Second question: When exactly should be begin telling our story? Well, if you haven't yet begun, why not begin at the dinner table with your family – or with a study group at church – people with whom you are familiar and comfortable.

To all of this, may I suggest that our story should include what Jesus has done for us personally. This really requires more of our time and thought. But it will be time well spent. Certainly, we have all been blessed abundantly. For me, this would include parents and family who loved me and sacrificed for me and saw that I received a good education. It would include good health and happiness with a lovely wife and three wonderful children and seven grandchildren. Add to this his care for me while serving several years in the Air Force; also our church, our friends, good health, healing, care givers, doctors and nurses, medicine, and long life.

We all have been blessed with freedoms and comforts. And what about our intellect and the time and the talents he has given us, our jobs and the abilities to perform them well.

This is pretty much my story. What's yours?

Now let's practice telling our stories to our loved ones and friends so that we'll be ready and excited to tell others as God gives us opportunity.

One final thought: let's never forget that everything we have is a gift from God. Everything!!

WHY ME LORD?

R onald Reagan once said to a friend over coffee at the White House that there were three things that most concerned him about growing old. "What might those be?" asked his friend. "First" said the president, "your memory goes." After a brief pause, a frown appeared upon his brow. Then, he continued, "I seem to have forgotten the other two."

Boy! Can I relate to that! There are times when I can clearly recall events from the distant past. But, there are other times when I can't remember the names of some of you, my friends, whom I have known for years. Go figure!

But there is one whose name we must never forget, isn't there?" A few weeks ago Pastor Jost spoke to us of David's Psalm 34:1 "His praise shall continually be on our mouth." Does that not say to us that we should always be alert for opportunities to praise our Lord and speak of him to others? I think so.

Lee Strobel, author of the best seller, The Case for Christ, urges Christians to follow Peter's counsel to be ready and willing to stand up for what we believe, and do it with gentleness and reverence (1 Peter 3:15). It seems Peter is saying to me, "David, stop and think for a while of all the blessings God has bestowed upon you and be ready to explain to anyone who asks what God has done for you. And practice your response so that it's on your lips when you need it."

So one evening last summer I went out on the porch and I tried to list all the blessings I could think of that came from my Lord. It took me over an hour before I finished, and I'm sure my list omitted a lot, probably many of which I have taken for granted.

Arthur Ashe, the late, gifted tennis superstar, had put his blessings in a proper perspective. When he contracted AIDS from a blood transfusion during heart surgery, he could have become very bitter, filled with self-pity, and asked himself, "Why me?" But he knew he could just as easily point to the many blessings he had from God and ask, "Why a Wimbledon championship? Why a beautiful, gifted wife, and a wonderful child?" Just to name a few.

If we all took the time to count the ways we have been blessed by our Lord, I believe we would have to ask ourselves that same question, "Why me, Lord?"

DO YOU KNOW JESUS?

O ne never knows what God may have in store for those who are anxious to speak to others of Jesus, but are hard-pressed to know how. Elizabeth was such a person. She prayed that God would help her with her witness. Her story was told in the December 2002 issue of Decision, a publication of the Billy Graham Evangelistic Association.

Not in her wildest dreams could Elizabeth have known what God had in mind for her when she pressed the "play" button on her answering machine.

The message was from a church secretary urgently seeking a priest to administer last rites to a dying man. The secretary left directions on how to get to the retirement home where the man was living

Elizabeth returned the call and explained that she had received the message by mistake. But she couldn't rest. She was certain God was calling her to action. With the driving instructions in hand – and praying all the way – Elizabeth raced to the retirement home where the dying man resided.

She asked the man's daughter for permission to talk to him, then sat at his bedside and asked, "Do you know Jesus?"

He stared at her.

"Daddy, she wants to tell you about Jesus," the daughter said. And so, Elizabeth did.

In the man's final hours, he heard the message of Jesus' love. When Elizabeth asked if he wanted to pray to accept Christ, the man squeezed his eyes shut, as if in prayer. He had seemed unable to speak, but after the prayer he summoned the strength to say,

"That was wonderful…thank you." A few hours later, the man peacefully passed away.

It seems that God had given Elizabeth the boldness and the courage to speak of Jesus' love.

ANOTHER LOOK AT THE LORD'S PRAYER

S everal years ago Laura and I drove back to my home town in Illinois for a weekend reunion with my brother and two sisters. River Forest is a small village a few miles west of Chicago; and I was pleased to see that little had changed. Our home at 302 Franklin Avenue was still nicely kept. Washington School was still there, and Keystone Field still had the three ball fields where I spent what seems like half my childhood.

The highlight of the weekend came on Sunday morning as we returned to worship at Trinity Lutheran Church where I had been baptized and confirmed. No sooner had we entered the narthex when I heard my name called. Turning about, whom should I see but Pastor Romoser, whom I had not seen for at least 30 years – now retired and in his eighties.

For a few minutes before worship began, we had a grand time getting caught up on families, jobs, and such. After the service he said to me "Come on, David, let's go see the torture chamber." He was referring to a small, glass-enclosed study room in the rear of the church tucked between the pastor's office and the choir room. It was here that he tried so hard every Saturday morning to teach me and three other classmates the Ten Commandments, the Creed, and the Lord's Prayer from Luther's Small Catechism. We also covered the sacraments and the Office of the Keys. I recall that there was a lot of memorization and recitation involved.

But I'm not so sure how much I really learned. There are portions of the Lord's Prayer, for example, that I have never really understood. This is especially true of the Second Petition, Your Kingdom Come. Luther teaches that this means that God's kingdom comes indeed without our prayer, of itself, and that it will come unto us also. We have all recited this petition hundreds and perhaps thousands of times; but I confess that there are often times when I really don't understand what I am saying.

Pastor Ron Lavin, former Pastor/Director of Evangelical Outreach for the Lutheran Church in America, shed some light on this for me while reading his book ABBA – Another Look at the Lord's Prayer. Pastor Lavin believes that, when we pray this petition, God's kingdom finds its way into our hearts and dwells there. He says it comes to us through people who love God and say so – that it comes to us through imperfect, sinful people like us – people who have faith in Jesus Christ and share their faith with us. He believes it comes to us in order to go through us to others.

What a beautiful thought!

WITNESSING - A STORY OF FEAR, COURAGE, AND LOVE

A minister once said something to me about evangelism that was unlike anything I had ever heard before. He maintained that, when we go out to minister to others in Jesus' name, we don't do it to save their souls, but to save our own. I don't think that I have ever thought of evangelism in quite that way. To make his point he told me a story of a young man who was converted to Christianity while a senior in high school. This is his story.

* * *

"I was a fresh, eager Christian; so when Tony Campolo came to our town to speak, I went to hear him. He was great! Then he asked us to sign up for his inner-city ministry in Philadelphia. We were really worked up and, when he finished, people were shouting and standing on the pews and clapping.

"OK gang," Dr. Campolo said, "Are you ready to go out there and tell 'em about Jesus?" "Let's go," we shouted. "Get on the bus," Tony shouted back.

We were clapping and singing as we left; but soon we began to drive further into the depths of the city. It got worse, and soon we stopped singing. Then the bus stopped before one of the worst-looking housing projects in the city. Tony jumped up and said "Alright gang, get out there and tell 'em about Jesus. I'll be back about five o'clock."

We made our way off the bus - slowly. We stood on the street corner, said a prayer, and then we spread out. I walked down a sidewalk and stopped before a huge tenement house. I gulped, said another prayer, and ventured inside. There was a terrible odor.

Windows were broken. No lights in the hall. I climbed a flight of stairs and heard a baby crying. I knocked on the door. "Who is it" said a loud voice inside. The door cracked open, and a woman holding a naked baby peered out at me. "What do you want?" she asked. I told her that I wanted to talk to her about Jesus. With that she began cursing me all the way down the hall, down the steps, and out to the sidewalk. I felt terrible. "Look at me," I said to myself. How in the world could somebody like me think I could tell people about Jesus?

Then I noticed a store on the corner. I walked in and remembered that the baby was wearing diapers; the mother was smoking a cigarette. So I bought a box of diapers and a pack of cigarettes. Then I walked back to the tenement house, climbed the stairs, gulped, and knocked on the door. When she opened it, I slid the box of diapers and the cigarettes inside. She looked at them, then at me, and said, "Come in."

I stepped into the dingy apartment. "Sit down" she commanded. I sat down on the old sofa and began to play with the baby; and I even put a diaper on. Then the woman offered me a cigarette. Even though I didn't smoke, I smoked and stayed there all afternoon talking, playing with the baby, and listening to the woman.

About four o'clock the woman looked at me and said "Let me ask you something. What's a nice boy like you doing in a place like this?" So I told her everything I knew about Jesus. It took about five minutes. Then she said, "pray for me and my baby, that we can make it out of here alive." I prayed.

That afternoon, when we were back on the bus, Tony asked, "Well gang, did any of you get to tell 'em about Jesus?" I stood up and I said, "I not only got to tell 'em about Jesus. I met Jesus. I went out to save somebody, and I ended up getting saved."

How's that for a story?

You know, there were a couple of things I noticed that surely helped this young man. Perhaps you noticed them, too. He listened to the woman. And he prayed – more than once.

A LIFE TRANSFORMED

The power of evangelizing is seen most clearly, I believe, with the telling of a story.

In order to illustrate this power, some time ago Pastor Mangiante used such a story in one of his sermons; and he has kindly allowed me to pass it on to you.

It's a story about an elderly monk, Athanasia, by name, who lived in the northern African desert during the third and fourth centuries. (He may have been named after St. Athanasius, Bishop of Alexandria, who at one time was thought to have written the Athanasian Creed.)

The story begins: A young traveler in need of shelter after a long day's journey stopped and asked Athanasia for a night's lodging. The elderly monk agreed and welcomed him into his home. While the two were dining, as was his custom, Athanasia read from his Bible, a rare and precious copy of the Gospels containing beautiful artwork and a jewel-studded cover. It was priceless in value.

Now it happens that the monk's young guest was, in fact, a thief; and of course, as Athanasia slept, the young man stole the Bible and hastened to a nearby town where he intended to sell it. He soon found a trader willing to buy on the condition that he might keep it for a short time to have it appraised. As it happened the appraiser he had in mind was none other than Athanasia, whom the trader thought would be a good judge of the book's value.

When Athanasia saw the Bible in the hands of the trader, all he said was "Oh yes, it is a rare and precious book and worth a great deal of money. Satisfied, the trader returned home and found the young cheat waiting anxiously. The exchange was made and, as he was leaving, the young man turned and asked the merchant how he had the book appraised. You can imagine the brigand's shock when the merchant replied "Well, I took it to an old monk who told me it was well worth what I was willing to pay for it. The thief was so upset that he gave back the trader's money and hurried away to return the stolen property to Athanasia and beg his forgiveness. But the monk simply replied "Oh no, the Bible is yours. I believe it a mortal sin to steal a Bible; so I give it to you. It is yours now."

The young man was overwhelmed by Athanasia's generosity and he stayed and cared for the old monk during his last years. Having experienced the forgiveness that Jesus Christ offers, he remained in the area and was loved by all who came into contact with him. His life was transformed forever.

CHRIST'S GIFT OF PRAYER

To have been chosen by Jesus to follow him the last three years of his life must have been an awesome experience for his disciples. Every day they were able to observe firstand the kind of man he was. They witnessed every day his ministry of love and mercy, his healings, his miracles, and teachings. Their's was an intimate relationship with him. They got to know him as no one else did.

As his chosen people, we too, can follow him and learn from him. He has left us with the Holy Spirit to teach, counsel, guide and equip us to witness of him to our world as his first grads did in their world some two thousand years ago. And we have the Bible, God's inspired word, to help us understand fully his purpose for us.

For several weeks now we have been contemplating these qualities that made Jesus who he is – love, obedience, service, and the like. Now let us reflect on another such virtue of his we might try to emulate in our outreach. That would be prayer – perhaps one of his most precious gifts.

He has even taught us how to pray. We call it the Lord's Prayer. He says to "pray in this way":

> Our Father in heaven, Hallowed be your name,
> Your kingdom come, Your will be done
> On earth as it is in heaven.
> Give us this day our daily bread. Forgive us our
> sins as we forgive those Who sin against us.

Save us from the time of trial, And deliver us from evil. For the kingdom, the power, and the glory are yours, now and forever. Amen.

For an in depth understanding of each petition in our Lord's Prayer, may I recommend to you a reading of Dr. Martin Luther's Small Catechism. For example, at the very outset of the prayer, you will notice how the Lord first addresses "Our Father" in heaven. By this, Dr. Luther means that God wants us to believe he is truly our Father, and we are truly his children – and also that, as the head of our family, we can boldly and with complete confidence teach this prayer to our children.

When you think about it or, as we say, meditate upon it, there seems to be little more that needs to be said about prayer. Our Lord's Prayer pretty much covers it all.

Scripture, however, does encourage us in many other ways to enhance our prayer ministry. For example: always pray in God's name; pray without ceasing; pray with thanksgiving; pray for God's will to be done, not ours; and when possible, find a quiet place to pray without distractions. Jesus often sought such solitude to be alone with his Father.

FORGIVENESS

How good are you at forgiving? If you are anything like me, there is plenty of room for improvement. I'm just not very good at it. And that concerns me because I believe forgiveness ranks right up there with love and obedience and service, as one of Jesus' virtues that we should be trying to imitate as we strive to become more like him.

I have read in the Bible that it's best "to first go to God for advice .... it's a good idea to talk to him in prayer and listen to him in his Word."

So that's what I did; and I discovered that Scripture is a veritable gold mine of information about forgiveness. Let's have a look.

* Jesus teaches us about prayer. (Mt 6:9) He says, pray like this: ".... and forgive us our sins, as we forgive those who sin against us." Sound familiar?
* Oh, what joy for those whose disobedience is forgiven, whose sin is put out of sight. (Psalm 32) (Romans 7)
* If you forgive those who sin against you, your heavenly Father will forgive you.

But if you refuse to forgive others, your Father will not forgive you. (Mt 14:15)

* Well then, should we keep on sinning so that God can show us more and more of his wonderful grace? Of course not!
* He was handed over to die because of our sins; and he was raised to life to make us right with God. (Romans 4:6-8)

* We read in Luke 23:34 as Jesus forgives his murderers. He says, "Father, forgive them for they don't know what they are doing."
* But, when you are praying, first forgive anyone you are holding a grudge against, so that our Father in heaven will forgive your sins, too. (Mark 11:25)
* Do not seek revenge or bear a grudge against a fellow Israelite, but love your neighbor as yourself. I am the Lord. (Leviticus 19:18)
* Love prospers when a fault is forgiven. (Proverbs 17:9)

Yes, love and forgiveness are good companions. It's hard to be good at one without being good at the other.

I believe a review of what Scripture has to say about all of this has helped me in what has, otherwise been a futile effort on my part toward building forgiveness into my character.

In closing, I just want to add that, for any of you who are finding it difficult to forgive, it might help to recall some of Scripture's roll models. The last chapter of Genesis, for example, records the beautiful story of Joseph's loving forgiveness of his brothers who conspired to kill him. Joseph explained to them, "You intended to harm me; but God intended it for good….."

The book of Acts relates the story of Stephen, the first Christian martyr, who was killed by members of the Jewish high counsel who feared their evil motives might be exposed. While he was praying for their forgiveness, they stoned him to death.

The New Testament is replete with tales of the apostles Peter and Paul and others who so often subjected themselves to dangers, imprisonment and, in some instances to a grisly death, as they courageously carried the Good News of Jesus Christ to unbelievers around the world.

THE GREATEST OF THESE

We are on a mission. By "we", I mean you and I - all of us together. Our mission is to try, as hard as we can, to learn as much as we can about Jesus — not just to learn about him — but to really *know* him — to have an intimate relationship with him, just as he had with his disciples during the three years they were together. We want to become as much like him as humanly possible. What can be better than that?

Last month, we meditated on the concept of bringing great joy to our Father (Mathew 3:17). In his letter to the Philippians written while in a Roman prison, Paul expressed the joy he felt in his relationship with Christ. Such is the joy we can also experience as we get to know him, as Paul did. The month before last we considered Jesus' obedience to his Father, even going so far as dying for us on the cross. We, in turn, are to obey the commands Jesus gives us to go and make new disciples and teach them to do likewise (Matthew 25:19-20). Looking Back, I feel somewhat uneasy about not beginning this article by upholding love as, first and foremost, the characteristic of Jesus which we might seek to embrace. After all, God is love; and he commands us to love others — even our enemies. In his first letter to the Corinthians, we find Paul's analysis of love, which are, in my mind, some of the most beautiful verses in all of Scripture (v.v. 1-13).

The apostle John, thought by some to be the apostle of love, picks up on this theme in his first pastoral letter to several gentile congregations: "Dear friends," he writes, "let us continue to love one another, for love comes from God. Anyone who loves is a child of God. But anyone who does not love does not know God, for God is love." John was thought to have been one of Jesus' closest and most loved disciples. How grand it is that we can treasure John's thoughts and his love words written here!

When we love, we become more like Christ.

JESUS' COMMANDS

As a boy growing up in River Forest, Illinois just west of Chicago, I was an avid baseball fan of the Chicago White Sox; and my idol was Luke Appling, the Sox shortstop. He didn't know it at the time, but I had already decided I was going replace him when he retired and entered the Hall of Fame. Yep, the Sox had nothing to worry about because I was going to be just as great as Luke had been.

Most all of us had someone we idolized when we were growing up. It might have been a star athlete, a favorite teacher, maybe a pastor, or even a movie star or singer. But, for whatever reason, things seldom worked out quite the way we planned.

Could the reason be that our plans were not always in keeping with what Jesus had in mind for us? Jesus' disciples had plans of their own. Peter and Andrew made their living as fishermen. So did James and John. Matthew found wealth as a tax collector. But, when Jesus told these men to follow him, that's exactly what they did. They obeyed him. Their mission was to go and make disciples and teach these new disciples to obey the commands He had given them (Mt 28:19-20). And so it is with us if we are to become Jesus' disciples.

But they had the advantage of being his hand-picked recruits. Indeed, it would be their privilege to be with him and have him for their own for three years to receive his teachings and witness his miracles first hand.

Does that mean Jesus has left us on our own? Of course not! He has left us with God's inspired Word, the Bible, and with select ministers to preach his Word from the pulpit every week and to teach us through small group Bible study meetings during the week. And what a privilege it has been to be able to learn from others of our Christian family during these small group studies!

God has also left us with one of his most precious gifts, his gift of time - time to read his Word and meditate upon it. May God forbid that we would waste any time he gives us!.

I am so thankful that he has given me the time and the opportunity to write these articles every month, because it constantly sends me back to Scripture to understand fully what he has done for me and what he expects from me in return.

Simply said, I believe he wants me to obey his commands, most especially his command to love and to try to reach out to others and make him known to them - to make more disciples for him and thereby grow his kingdom.

That's quite a challenge; but he has told us that all things are possible through him.

YOU ARE ALWAYS WELCOME

B efore my recent release from the hospital, I was given a handful of forms to complete and sign. One was rather perplexing, asking what method of teaching worked best for me. Several options were offered, each with a box to check if I felt it applied to me; e.g. reading, listening, demonstration, practice. I was tempted to add another, my wife; but I thought better of it.

After some thought, I checked the boxes for listening, demonstration, and practice. But I also believe that yet another method might have been offered; -- visual aids. When you think about it, visual aids are often used to facilitate the learning process; and they can be used in a variety of ways.

As Christians, for example, many of us, perhaps without even giving it a thought, demonstrate our faith without even saying a word. How often, for example, do you notice someone with a cross hanging around their neck or pinned to their lapel? Simple acts of kindness or encouragement can work wonders, such as applauding the singing of our children's choirs and their music directors during worship, or visiting a shut in, or giving a recent visitor a cookie patrol bag filled with a Bible and a dozen freshly-baked cookies. Or when we pray before a meal in one of our favorite restaurants, and even asking diners at a nearby table if there is anyone they would like to include in our prayers. All kinds of ways to express our faith to others.

I recently had occasion to thank our good friend, Harold Yoos, for one of the nicest gifts we had ever received. It's a framed, handmade display of three crosses he had affixed to a gray shingle left over after our old bell tower had been torn down many years ago. What made it so beautiful was the simplicity which Harold had so artfully represented Christ's sacrifice for us on the cross.

Another of God's beautiful visual aids which we treasure is a framed painting of Warner Salmon's Christ at Heart's Door, showing our Lord knocking on the door of an unbeliever's heart, hoping to be invited in. But the door can only be opened from within, for there is no handle on the outside of the door.

Jesus wants earnestly to be invited into our hearts so that he can abide in us and befriend us because he loves us so. I can't but wonder how nice it would have been if the artist had painted yet another picture showing the door slightly ajar as Christ is shown seeking entry and asking,

"Is anybody home? May I please come in?" then, hearing the owner's reply, "Oh, yes, Lord, please do come in. You are always welcome."

Sadly, some may never open the door to their hearts. But, of one thing we can be certain. Christ will never stop knocking.

FAMILY

THE STETH-O-SCOPE

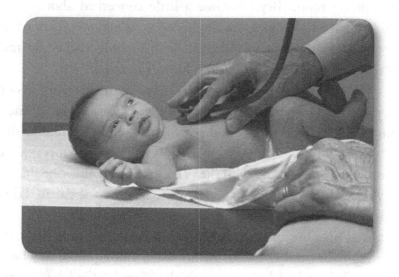

Some years ago I received a letter postmarked Santa Ana, California; and the return address label bore the names: Mr. and Mrs. Harold McDonnel, Fullerton, California. I knew of nobody named McDonnel nor, for that matter, did I know anyone in Santa Ana or Fullerton, CA. Enclosed in the envelope was a beautiful, hand-written note from Anna Yoos McDonnel, daughter of George and Georgina Yoos, longtime members of St. Paul's many years ago.

Unknown to me, Anna is one of many former members who still receive copies of our monthly newsletter, *Chimes*; and when it's delivered, she says she reads every page immediately - and adds that "St. Pauls is very dear to my heart."

She also mentioned that my evangelism article caught her eye, adding that she thought it a "wonderful story." How very kind of her to say so! The story, as I recall, had to do with how easy it is for some people, especially children, to speak of Jesus to others. I was referring specifically to my granddaughter, Bryn, who was three years old at the time. Her mother, Michele, had taken Bryn to her pediatrician for a checkup. When the doctor entered the examining room, Bryn became a little concerned about "that thing" that was hanging around his neck. When he explained to Bryn that he was going to listen to her heart, she reached up and whispered in his ear: "You know, Jesus is in there."

The point that I was trying to make with this story about Bryn was how wonderful it would be if we adults could set aside our inhibitions and speak to others of Jesus as easily as children do.

Even if I say so myself, that is an enchanting story; but I thought what Anna did with the s t o r y was very nice. She shared it. As Devotions Chairman of her WELCA group, she shared this story with some 45 ladies at their monthly meeting.

And imagine our surprise when, on Easter morning this past Spring, Laura and I saw our names listed among those to whom Easter flowers had been given to the glory of God by, -- you guessed it – Anna Yoos McDonnel. And she adds in parentheses: "I enjoy Dave's columns each month and I share them." Saying kind things seems to come easily to this fine lady.

Jesus' half-brother, James, tells us in his first chapter that we should humbly accept the word God has planted in our hearts. Then he adds that we should not just listen to God's word, but we must also do what it says. I believe that you at St. Paul's are doing God's word, and that you are doing it by the way you live and by the way you become a blessing to others. I'm referring to those of you who,

- as Church Council members, give of your time and your talents by managing the business affairs of St. Paul's;

- teach our children about Jesus;
- go into the world to places like Bosnia, New Orleans, and Biloxi - and many others of you who, through your Benevolence giving, reach out to the storm victims in Haiti, Chile, Japan and Joplin;
- visit the sick and shut-ins;
- helped our immigrant families acclimate to life in America;
- share their time and talents as members of our choirs and chorales;
- serve as Social Ministry Team members reaching out and doing for many, many people in need;
- share their time and talents as shawl sharers and as Needle and Thread quilt makers; teach and serve our youth through Rejoice school and Joyful House;

I could go on and on; but I think you get my drift. Just a word of caution: Let's not get too puffed up about this. It's my understanding that we are only able to do these good things through the power of the Holy Spirit.

So, you see, Anna: there are many here at St. Paul's who are *doing* and *sharing*, just like you.

They must have been cut from the same bolt of kindness that you were.

Before closing let me say that I hesitate to write about someone without first getting that person's permission to do so. When I reviewed this with Anna, she gave me her approval, asking only if I might add a passage from 2nd Corinthians 1: 3-4 that served as something of personal mission statement by which her parents and she tried to live their lives:

"Blessed be the God and Father of our Lord Jesus Christ, the Father of mercies and the God of all consolation, who Consoles us in all our affliction, so that we may be able to console those who are in any affliction with the consolation with which we ourselves are consoled by God." (NRSV)

Now let us praise God for giving us these opportunities to serve him and others, and for enabling us as we strive to realize our potential as Christians. Praise God from whom all blessings flow; praise him all creatures here below; praise him above ye heav'nly host; praise Father, Son and Holy Ghost.

FISHERS OF MEN

To say that my son-in-law is an ardent fisherman would be an understatement. Bert loves to fish. And he's very good at it. When he was just a boy, his father spent a lot of time with him on the water, teaching him all there was to know about handling a boat, and all about lures, bait, reels, outriggers, and such -- and, most importantly, how to find fish.

Bert learned that birds hovering low over the water signaled fish below. The churning of the water's surface by bait fish was also a sure indicator that larger fish were lurking below. His equipment included an electronic fish finder that disclosed the location of schools of fish. (I thought this was cheating a little, and I told him so, but he kind of ignored me).

One day, while in the Bahamas, Bert took me and both of my sons, John and Andy, right to where the fish were. Our lines were in the water for less than a half hour before Andy landed a twenty-two pound grouper and, soon after, I hooked a fifteen pounder. Before the day was over, John reeled in a good-sized reef shark (which we released), and together, our catch for the day included a dozen yellow-tail snappers. Boy, did we eat good that night!

By now you have probably figured out where I'm going with this, so I'll get to the point.

For three years, Jesus taught his disciples how to become "fishers of men" -- and he taught them where to find the "fish." They didn't just hunker down at the water's edge and wait for the fish to come to them. They hit the road. Jesus went to the synagogues, and his disciples followed him to places like Gennesaret, Tyre, and Sidon, and to Cana, and Sychar, and Nain.

Along the way, his disciples learned their craft as he preached, and taught, and healed among the sick and the poor.

I don't know about you, but I've learned something from this "fishers of men" story. I've learned that I've been going about it the wrong way. You see, for some time now, I've been asking God to send me someone to whom I might tell my faith story. I'm all cocked and ready to go; but nothing seems to be happening. Where are all the "fish?"

Then it hit me. I can't just sit around and wait for something to happen. I've got to get off my rear end and make it happen. But I'm not sure just how to go about it. I could use something like that electronic fish finder Bert uses. And then I thought, Maybe, if I pray about it. Would you help me?

How about we make a deal? If you'll pray for me, then I'll do the same for you. Maybe together we can become pretty good fishermen.

YOUTH WITH A MISSION

M emories of our children and grandchildren sometimes grow dim with the passing of time, but one thing in particular remains clearly in my mind. When my granddaughter, Dale, was about three years old, she and I often played a game we called *I see something .... If*, for example, I chose the color blue, she would reply "the sky." Then she would come back with "I see something green," and I would respond, correctly, "a tree." She would think about this for a moment and then answer with a giggle, "no Pop, it's the grass."

What a difference the years can make!

Halawasa is a Christian summer camp located just outside Hammonton, New Jersey. Dale has enjoyed several summers at Halawasa, serving as a counselor for the past two. Over the years, she has made many lasting friendships with Christian youth.

Now age 19, she has embarked on a most incredible journey, traveling half way around the world to participate in a six-month discipleship training program sponsored by Youth With A Mission (YWAM). After two days travel last fall, she arrived in Townsville, Australia, a town some 700 miles north of Sydney, on the Coral Sea. I'd like to share with you how she relates, via e-mail, some of what is happening in her young life.

Sunday afternoon of the first week was devoted to orientation, followed the next day by what Dale described as "incredible worship." She had been praying that God would just "reach out and grab hold of her heart." And that's exactly what He did. "I found myself completely surrendering to my Lord once again," she reported.

Policies, procedures, and a history of the base were reviewed during the first week. Then the young people were informed that they would be divided into three teams of eight or nine persons each, and each team would be given a choice of one of three assignments for the final two months of their six month mission.

Option 1 was Palm Island, a small island some two hours off the Australian coast, where they would be working with indigent people. Option 2 would dispatch a team to Darwin, Australia, and then on to East Timor, a small island of the East Indies, also working with people living in extreme poverty. The third team, mostly girls, would be sent to Thailand to work primarily with prostitutes and women involved in sex trafficking. Dale had stated early on that she would go wherever she was needed, but secretly she hoped to be part of the Thailand team. And that's what she got.

Before going on, I should explain that Dale has her own way of describing just how excited she is about this mission. I counted seven "awesomes" in her first few e-mails, followed closely by five "incredibles", three "cools," and one "I'm having a blast."

Thursday night of the second week was the kickoff of Stable on the Strand, a week-long festival preparing for Christmas. (Strand is the Aussie's definition of "beach.") The youth b u s i e d themselves setting up an entire Bethlehem village on the strand. All of the Townsville churches joined in for this fun-time. Concerts were arranged, vendors and speakers invited, all with a view toward raising funds and enlisting volunteers for the youth mission. This was Dale's first "awesome" experience.

During the ensuing ten weeks of training, the teams were engaged in a wide range of activities: a full week of lectures, the theme being "Clear Conscience." By week's end, each person had an opportunity to stand up before the class and confess what God had laid on his or her heart that week. This enabled everyone to get to know one another "sooo well." Lots of crying, too.

Time was devoted to scripture study, talking about spiritual gifts, and Biblical truths such as "God is with me; I have nothing to fear" and "Christ made me beautiful, just the way I am."

One night was set aside for Outreach Prep, sharing faith stores and testimonies. Another of Dale's "awesome."

Two weeks were spent in a rain forest, a few miles removed from base – "an incredible time to really get to seek my Lord."

Time and space limit a more comprehensive coverage of the training. Let's move on to THAILAND.

Jan 11th: Arrived in Bangkok. More cultural orientation, touring temples and getting accustomed to transportation.

Jan 14th: Departed Bangkok for Mae Sot where we worked at an orphanage named Agape Children's Home, teaching English to some 100 kids from the Karen tribe and two other hill tribes. Lots to do: running English camps, doing skits, throwing birthday parties, worshiping, giving testimonies, prayers for healing, etc. One morning, a handful of elderly women trickled in and asked for more prayer. Many whom we encountered had never seen a white person.

Jan 28th: Set out northward to Chang Mai, close to the China/Laos border, where we ministered to yet another hill tribe orphanage, whose inhabitants had been subjected to various forms of exploitation and human slavery. It was here that the team prepared packages containing Bibles to be smuggled into China.

Feb 10th: A 12-hour bus ride south, across mountainous terrain, to Pattaya, where we will be working with bar women, inviting them to English class and Bible study. My team feels this is where God wants them to do something HUGE. As an all-girls team, we will be ministering to bar women and prostitutes, distributing bags of rice to needy families, playing games, singing songs with children of the Pattaya slum ministry, and washing their hair with a special lice shampoo.

Feb 20th: Scheduled to return to Bangkok for a few days of debriefing.

Feb 27th: Return to Townsville.

I feel certain that Dale would agree that it was not so much what she was doing in Thailand as it was about what the Holy Spirit was doing through her and her team.

Just imagine! With prayer and the nurturing of the Holy Spirit and some intentional follow- up by other teams, God's Word and his glory will now be passed forward to a new generation by those whom Dale and her team have touched.

My granddaughter continues to ask us to pray for her, and her team, and for the people they have encountered.

BLOWN OPPORTUNITIES

I 'd like to share with you a story about something that has happened to me, and I hope it will never happen to you.

Laura and I head for Florida every winter to visit our daughter, Linda, and her family. Over the years, I've become pretty good friends with John, a neighbor of theirs. John and I have quite a lot in common. We're both retired. We have both served in the Air Force. And both of us are Republicans. He doesn't play golf, but so far I've been able to overlook this particular flaw in his character.

John has a dog, a mixed breed who answers to the name of Max, and every morning he takes Max for a walk up to the beach – only a short block and a half away. And often John would stop by and ask, if I'd like to join him.

Well, soon after, on a beautiful Sunday morning, I took John up on his offer, and the two of us, with Max at our heels, headed for the beach. As we sat on a bench overlooking the beautiful Atlantic, John asked if all of us were going to church. I said we were and we would be leaving about 10:30. The bad part was that I failed to recognize this splendid opportunity God had placed right in my lap to invite John to come along with us. I didn't think a whole lot about it until we returned from church. John was out in his front yard and, as we got out of the car, he called over and asked how the church service had been.

Now you see, right here God had given me yet another chance to invite. But did I pick up on this? No! Instead of saying something like "The service was fine, John. You would have enjoyed it. I'll tell you what! Why don't you come along with us next week?" all I came up with was something stupid. "The service was fine, John. At least, I stayed awake." Sometimes, I'm just too darn glib for my own good.

I didn't feel too badly about this until later, when Linda phoned and told Laura that John and his wife asked if they could go to church with them. So the story had a happy ending, but certainly not because of anything I said or did. God must have been very disappointed in me that day for dropping the ball as I did. John just might have been one of those people – and there is a vast number of them - longing for someone to invite them to church.

As I think about it now, I am reminded of the scripture reading that cautions us to be alert, or be prepared. I believe it is used in the context that we need to be ready for that time when Christ comes to us again, that he may come like "a thief in the night." But doesn't it tell us also that we need to be alert to those opportunities to invite people to church with us? I think so!

If there is an upside to this story, I will never ever let an opportunity like this pass me by again. And I hope you won't, either.

LEARNING DISABILITIES

A utism is defined as a severe disorder of brain function marked with problems with social contact, intelligence, and language. And it's a lifelong disorder that interferes with the ability to understand what is seen, heard and touched. It can cause profound problems with personal behavior and the ability to relate to others. Research estimates that over two million special education teachers are needed now to help autistic children learn how to relate to the world.

You may be familiar with this disease; but I knew little about it until I viewed a segment on *60 Minutes* a few weeks ago that featured the work and life of Steve Jobs, the recently- deceased CEO of Apple – the man who has introduced to the world the iPad and many other technological devices which are making life easier and more enjoyable for people around the world.

The TV show focused on how the iPad is being used to teach autistic children how to overcome their disability. If you saw the program, you may have been touched, as I was, to see the joy brought to their faces as the iPad helped them communicate with their parents and family, their friends, and their teachers. Can you imagine what a difference these instructors are making in the lives of these children?

While visiting recently with relatives and friends in the Chicago area, we met such a person. A pretty young lady, somewhere in her mid to late twenties, I'm guessing. Her name is Beth, and she teaches autistic children and others with special education needs.

After dinner one evening my ninety- year old sister, Jane,

and Beth had time to get acquainted; and Jane immediately took a liking to her young companion. After a while, however, Jane chanced on the fact that Beth had a special learning need of her own. To her dismay, Jane discovered that Beth had never learned about Jesus. No Sunday school exposure! No Bible Study! Nothing! Jane thought: "How can that be?" But further discussion confirmed what she had heard and, as you might imagine, she was devastated. But, right then and there, Jane resolved that she was going to do something about it. She just had to figure out a way to bring this young woman from ground zero to an understanding and acceptance of Jesus Christ as her Lord and Savior. (to be continued next month)

JANE'S FAITH STORY

L et me tell you about my sister, Jane, and her resolve to testify of Jesus to her young friend, Beth, who for the first twenty-five plus years of her life had never known anything about Jesus.

As the matriarch of the Jonathan family, Jane had long felt the need to tell the story of her faith in God. As with many of you, she and her husband, Dick, had witnessed of their faith by the way they lived, loved, and worshiped. But now she felt the need to express her faith in writing so as to have something tangible she could pass on to her family and loved ones – and especially now to her new-found friend, Beth.

Jane's story consists of eight type-written pages – obviously too much to include in this article; so I'll try to hit some of the highlights. After much thought and prayer that the Holy Spirit would give me a hand with this, I decided to begin with Genesis and end with Jesus' resurrection, because that's pretty much the way Jane tells it.

She writes first of God's creation – what she refers to as "a story of God's wondrous works." Her close: Jesus' resurrection – His victory over death and His promise of eternal life with Him in heaven for all believers. The rest of her narrative transports her readers through many of the Old Testament stories, which she very much enjoyed, and, on to the New Testament, beginning with the four Gospels.

Jane encourages Beth and her readers to take in the Genesis story of God's creation so as to understand the wonder of God's works. Described at some length is the story of Adam and Eve and their ill-fated encounter with Satan. Her narrative continues with the stories of Noah and the flood, the righteousness and trust of Abraham and Sarah, Isaac and his offspring, Moses, who, with God's guidance, led the Israelites through the wilderness and on toward the Holy Land. Mention is also made of the Ten Commandments, Jacob, and Esau, the twelve tribes of Israel, and Joseph and his influence on the Pharaoh and his household.

My sister enjoyed these Old Testament stories and especially recommended to her readers the stories she loved of Ruth and Naomi, of Esther and, of course, the Psalms, and the prophecies, all of which are to be fulfilled by Jesus in the New Testament.

The very first paragraph of our Apostles Creed gets right to the heart of the matter: her belief in our Triune God. She writes of the peace and happiness she has found through reading and learning from God's word, adding "it is my prayer that you will also have God in your hearts."

Not knowing quite where to go from there, Jane asked herself how her faith in God may have had its beginning. After some thought, she realized it may have taken root years ago when, as a child, she was told in Sunday school that Jesus loved little children. And then, a few years later, she learned in Confirmation studies that God loved her so much that he gave His only Son to die for her on the cross, and that all she had to do was believe in Him, and she would live with Him here and hereafter in heaven. (John 3:16)

Of chief importance are the Good News stories of the Gospel writers – Jesus' birth, His parables and teachings, His ministries and His many miracles and, of course, His terrible suffering and death on the cross; and finally, His joyous victory over death on Easter morning.

Jane strongly encouraged Beth and her readers to read the book of Acts to discover how Paul and Jesus' disciples spread the word of Jesus as our Savior, underscoring the truth that our faith in Jesus, and this alone, assures us of eternal life with Him in heaven.

You may have noticed that Jane often uses the word *encourage* in her testimony. And so it is with the word *love*. Both words, she believes, are crucial to living as a Christian. She closes by saying to Beth and her loved ones that "I love you so very much that I give you this Triune God to hold in your hearts.... Please read God's Word and know that it is the true story of God's love for us."

At age 90, Jane is up in years. But I failed to mention that some twenty years earlier she had also lost her vision due to macular degeneration. But she wasn't about to let anything stand in her way. She realized that God, through His bounteous grace, had given her time to tell others of her faith.

It's been quite some time now since Jane last spoke with Beth, so she knows little of how her faith story influenced her friend. But Jane is not discouraged. She is certain that the seed she has planted will be nurtured by God and that, in His time, it will grow.

That's the way it happens here at St. Paul's, my church, and at all the other places of worship, isn't it? Every time we welcome a newcomer into our midst, we are saying, in effect, "We love you, and we would like you to come again and become a part of our church family as we, together, seek to grow God's kingdom."

GETTING TO KNOW JESUS .... REALLY WELL

B irthdays are happy times, aren't they? Especially for kids. Parties and presents and, of course, cake and candles. Two of our grandsons, Drew and Jeff, celebrate their birthdays in January. One year, when they were just little tykes, they both had to be reminded to make a wish before they blew out the candles. And they had to keep their wish a secret, too; otherwise, their wish wouldn't come true. Those are the rules.

Remembering back to when I was their age, I probably wished for a new toy, or a sled, or maybe a baseball mitt; but, as we grow older, our wishes change somewhat, don't they? As a teenager, I can recall how I hoped and prayed for good marks on my SATs so that I could get into a good college. As a young adult, getting a good job was high on my wish list, and, a few years later, finding the perfect wife – and raising a family. And all the while most of what I wished for was for me – and, of course, my family -- success on the job, good health and happiness for all of us.

And then came retirement. Almost without realizing it, I came to feel that what I really wanted most now was to get to know my Lord Jesus better. It's a little late in life, but now I'm beginning to spend more time with my Bible and attending some of our small group Bible studies at church – something I should have begun years ago.

We are often reminded that we are to be good stewards of everything God has entrusted to us. Not just our treasures and talents, but the *time* he has given us, as well. Here at St. Paul's, what better way to use our time than to spend it in Bible study?"

What's in it for those who attend? How about great fellowship, a chance to be with some really nice people and get to know them well? How about a chance to get better acquainted with our Lord and Savior? - all of this while listening to Scripture explained in a way that will enhance your understanding of God's word.

THIS LITTLE GIFT OF MINE....LET IT SHINE

My granddaughter, Bryn, and I had just left Rita's with our frozen cups of Italian ice. I pushed the power button on the car CD player and, to my delight, some children were singing *"This Little Light of Mine, Let it Shine, Let it Shine."* I thought what a neat way to introduce our Wednesday morning discussion group gathering - and also a way to begin this article for *Chimes."*

Have you ever thought about the gifts that you have from God? We've been doing just that in our small group discussion on Wednesday mornings. Using the Bible as our guide, we encouraged each other to share with the group how God has gifted them; and then each of us was asked to remark upon any gifts we saw in others of the group. And what an eye-opening experience that was!

Some spoke of others with the gift of teaching; still others with the gift of compassion.

One person made it her practice to visit the sick and shut-ins with her pet poodle. Another was cited for his gift of design and carpentry. Love of music and choir singing was a blessing shared by another group member. And yet another was seen as simply giving of herself to God's service. Courage, Christian parenting, needlepoint, and organization were other blessings voiced by the group.

In the 12th chapter of Romans Paul appeals to each of us to present our bodies as a living sacrifice... and be transformed by the renewing of our minds so that we may discern the will of God. I believe that's what was happening to us in our discussion group. Our minds were being transformed in a way that we might discover those gifts with which God had blessed us, and how we might use them to serve Him.

During our discussion, my mind was drawn to the group down the hall of the study house – our Needle and Thread ladies, and how they have mastered their talents of creating beautiful quilts to be given to the needy. I wonder if they realize that this may be one of the "purposes" God had in mind for each of them.

It seems to me that there is one common thread that can be found in all of these gifts. It's the gift of time, one of God's most precious gifts to each of us. Every time we see a child baptized we are reminded that we should "let our light so shine before others so that they may see our good works and glorify our Father in heaven." Rick Warren reminds us in his book that our purpose in life is to glorify God, using the gifts He has given us.

THE GIVER OF GOOD

I t's been over six years since I first introduced you to our granddaughter, Dale. She had just completed a six month Discipleship Training program sponsored by YWAM (Youth With A Mission) that took her to Australia and then on to Thailand to work with young Thai women who had fallen victims to sex traffickers. By means of Bible Study and English language training Dale and seven others from around the world were able to equip these Thai girls with job skills so they would no longer have to rely on their bodies to make a living.

Dale is twenty-four now and is a graduate of Messiah College in Grantham, Pennsylvania.

Her father, our oldest son John, shared with us a very nice faith story she wrote recently about what's going on in her life now. It is based on Romans 12:1-2; and she has titled it *The Giver of Good*.

Utilizing "Facebook" technology Dale has reached out to more than 2,000 new "friends" with whom she has also shared her story. Please read on.

*   *   *

I've been going through this time in my life during which God has asked me to spend more time with Him – to focus on Him – and put him first in my life again. It has been *so good* for my soul.

My experience has been that, when God starts to work on your heart, it definitely hurts.

Kinda like working out for the first time in a while. You're sore. But, the more I stay with it, the less it hurts and the better my body feels. Well, I feel it's the same way with the Lord. Maybe it's because, at first, I'm not sure just where he's headed. But I *do* know he's headed for good. Often it doesn't seem that way until I see the good in what he's doing; and this becomes a time for celebrating!

God often teaches with simple truths – truths He brings into a new light even though we've been subjected to them a thousand times. This past week God has been reminding me that He is *the giver of good*. All good things *do* come from the Lord. Yeah, yeah! I know you've heard it all before. But, I seriously believe all *good things come from the Lord*. Scripture underscores this fact time after time: Psalms 34:8; Mark 10:18; John 10:11; 1 Timothy 4:4, to mention a few.

This simple revelation has made this a seriously spectacular time for me. Honestly, making praise a daily habit has allowed me to see God in everything. It's been so cool to see something good happen, and then turn around and realize that it came from God. By simply acknowledging him as the giver of all things good, I have been consistently overwhelmed at seeing His hand at work in my life. He is everywhere.

Let me tell you of a simple revelation I had tonight at powerhouse.* Sometime, I have thoughts like: "I need to go to worship because it's going to make me feel better." And it causes me to question my motives for wanting to go to worship. I didn't want it to be like worship becomes my quick fix; so I was praying about it, and God answered with this: "We were created to worship our Maker." As beings made in the likeness of God, we were created to praise Him with our lives. It's no wonder we desire to be in his presence and worship Him. It's what we were created to do.

So live on! See God as something unexpected! Be encouraged

because the Giver of Good is definitely at work in your life. (*Powerhouse is the name of Dale's Bible Study.)

- -

Well done, Dale! It appears to me that you have been meditating quite a bit with your God – and that you have developed it into a kind of art form. I should imagine that you find quite a bit of peace in spending time with God as you do. But what I find extraordinary about your story is not so much the story itself, but the realization that you have connected with over 2,000 others through its telling. Is that awesome, or what? Some of your "friends" may read it, then set it aside and move on with their lives. But I suspect many more will take it to heart and then pass it on. Who knows how many times your faith story will be retold? And who knows how many others will be moved to spend more time with their Lord and write their own story? These would be those – the "good soil about whom Jesus speaks in Mark 4:20. Grampa Page

A CARE PACKAGE

A letter from home was always special when I was serving in the Air Force years ago, especially when it came with a "care package" of Mom's homemade cookies. I'm sure the same is true today of the men and women serving in the Armed Forces.

A church member/friend of our daughter, Linda, recently received a letter from her son, Sean, who is serving in Afghanistan. Included with the letter was a list of men and women serving in his platoon... The list was circulated to church members asking if they would like to send a "care package" to one of those whose name appeared on the list. Linda selected the name of Bryan Harrison.

A few weeks later Bryan received Linda's letter and package containing a bevy of items most needed by troops overseas. Her package included socks, underwear, Power Bars, M and M's, Jolly Ranchers, Trail Mix, pretzels, body wash, two magazines, two paperbacks, a soldier's Bible, an inspirational book mark, playing cards, Portals of Prayer, gum, a baseball cap, zip lock bags, and chap stick.

Hers was a four paragraph letter; but it was her last paragraph that I felt was rather touching : "....We can't pretend to know what you are going through or feeling while serving our country, but please know how much we appreciate your service for all of us. You will be in our prayers.

You know, I have never written to a complete stranger before, but I pray all the time for people I don't know. May Christ's blessings be with you!

As a P.S. she added "My two kids said that I should confess how I happened to select your name from the list of thirty soldiers in your platoon; so here goes: I once had a huge crush on Harrison Ford. There! I did it. Oh, well!

A CARING CONVERSATION

O ur son, John, informed me recently that he, his wife, Laura, and their 15-year- old son, Drew, were studying the book of Proverbs during their evening meals. I thought: *Good for them.* That sounded to me like a nice, caring conversation.

It had been years, perhaps decades, since I had read Proverbs, and I was curious as to why they selected this particular book. So I checked it out. Sure enough, right there in the introduction the reader was told that Proverbs was a textbook for teaching people how to live godly lives. Solomon's purpose was to impart wisdom, discipline, and moral truth to young people who might greatly benefit from his wise words.

Call it what you like, but I believe that, when a family gathers in their home to read and discuss God's word, they are witnessing of their faith to each other. Indeed, evangelism can, and perhaps should, begin at home. Not only were Drew's parents engaged in a caring conversation with him, but they were also telling him, albeit in a rather oblique way, just how much they loved him.

In Matthew 10:11 Jesus sends out his twelve disciples, instructing them to search for a "worthy" person. Now I ask you, who is more worthy than our own children or, for that matter, our grandchildren. And let's not overlook our godchildren.

Let's take a look at a few of Solomon's pearls of wisdom as found in the book of Proverbs: 1:10 - "My child, if sinners entice you, turn your back on them!"

2:1 – "My child, listen to what I say ...." (The word *listen* appears in many of the proverbs.

Could it be that Solomon may be asserting that it's not enough to simply *hear* God's word, but that we must listen and try to understand?")

3:27 – "Do not withhold good from those who deserve It …."

12:14 – "…. hard work brings rewards."

17:9 – "Love prospers when a fault is forgiven …."

19:16 – "Keep the commandments…."

20.7 – "The godly walk with integrity; …." (This one may require some discussion to help youngsters understand.)

22:9 – "Blessed are those who are generous, because they feed the poor."

These are but a few I thought were special. Can you imagine what our world would be like if these words of advice were given to all children when they reached an age of understanding? Looking back, I wish that Laura and I had done for our children what John and his Laura have done for their son, Drew. I think they got it right.

GOD'S MYSTERIOUS WAYS

Our daughter Linda had just dropped her two children off at school one morning when she noticed in her rear view mirror a car rapidly approaching and weaving from side to side. Due to road construction in the right lane, she was unable to avoid being rear-ended. She stopped and stepped out to inspect the damage and asked the other driver, quite obviously under the influence, to follow her to a gas station just ahead where they could discuss the matter and exchange insurance information. He became most belligerent and, cursing at her, leaped back into his car and sped off, but not before Linda was able to grasp a piece of paper from her purse and write down his license plate number. Using her cell phone she then phoned the West Palm Beach police department to report the accident.

Some twenty minutes later the policewoman who had taken Linda's call arrived at the scene. Linda gave the officer the piece of paper with the recorded license number. Later that afternoon, the policewoman phoned Linda to report that, with the aid of the license number, the young driver had been apprehended.

But that's not the end of the story.

The following afternoon Linda received a phone call from the policewoman to say that she still had the piece of paper that Linda had given her. Linda told her that she really didn't need it – to which the officer replied that *she* needed it; for on the reverse side of the paper a Bible verse was written which Linda and her ten-year-old son, Jeffrey, had been rehearsing in the car, preparing him for his Chapel class that day. The policewoman confessed that yesterday had been a very difficult day for her, and Jeffrey's handwritten verse had helped her through the day. She asked Linda to thank Jeff and, of course, he thought that was pretty cool – like he had just helped track down a dangerous criminal.

Oh! The verse: Psalm 37: 7-9. "… Be patient and wait for the Lord to act; don't be worried about those who prosper or those who succeed in their evil plans. Don't give in to worry or anger; it only leads to trouble…."

The policewoman offered nothing further as to how this particular Bible passage had helped her, nor did Linda inquire. But she did have a sense that God's word must have had some kind of a calming effect on her.

At dinner that evening the family wondered to one another how this passage could have been so helpful. Perhaps the lady had a bitter argument with her husband before leaving for work – or maybe she had been passed over for a promotion which she had hoped for. In any event, God's counsel had been just the tonic the lady needed. And it had all come about as a result of something a young boy had written on a piece of paper, not having a clue as to how it might impact another person's life.

Sometimes God does use us in mysterious ways.

BLESSED TO BE A BLESSING

Working in partnership with Lutheran Social Ministry Refugee and Sponsorship Services NJ, St. Paul's opened its arms to a family of nine who fled the West African nation of Liberia to escape the ravages of civil war. For the past fifteen years, "home" for them had been a mud hut in a refugee camp in neighboring Ghana.

When Laura and I returned from our winter holiday in Florida, we were amazed at the volume of e-mails to be read, most of them relating to the flurry of activity arising from the arrival of our new friends on January 30th. We learned that over twenty people responded to Michele's appeal for volunteers to help with a myriad of tasks – all focused on aiding our refugee family with their transition to life in America. Organizing clothing drives, enrolling teen-age girls in high school, driving some to ESL (English Second Language) classes, scheduling blood tests, doctor appointments, dental and eye examinations, obtaining Social Security cards, arranging job interviews, grocery shopping, opening checking accounts, preparing a budget, and much, much more.

I think this says a lot about St. Paul's. We are, indeed, being true to our church motto: *Blessed to be a Blessing.* Let us thank God for giving us this opportunity, and also the people, the resolve, and the means to serve those who needed so much help. Paul puts it nicely in the sixth chapter of his letter to the Galatians, as he encourages us to bear one another's burdens, and not to grow weary of doing what is right.

Now, if I may, I'd like to tell you of another Lutheran church with an outreach story of its own. It happens to be the church to which our daughter and her family belong.

Working through LIRS (Lutheran Immigration and Refugee Services) in Baltimore, Faith Lutheran, West Palm Beach, Florida, has "adopted" a young mother, Christine and her son, Herman, natives of the small central African country of Burundi, yet another nation besieged by civil war that has exposed thousands to all manner of brutality and murder. When Herman was just one year old, Christine's husband, a doctor, was murdered in front of their home for refusing to treat the wounds of enemy soldiers. Four of Christine's siblings met a similar fate.

She and her son soon joined hundreds of other Burundis awaiting relocation from their war- torn nation. Eventually, they were sent to Burkina Faso, a small West African nation located adjacent to Ghana. It was there in Burkina Faso that Christine and Herman would spend the next seven years, living in a tent with more than a hundred other refugees. I really don't believe that any of us residing here in America can comprehend the horror and the deprivation these families have experienced these past decades in their native lands.

When Christine and Herman arrived in Florida, our daughter, Linda, was among the small group of Faith Lutheran members who welcomed them at Palm Beach International airport. Living accommodations had been arranged, and many church members gifted the newcomers with clothing, furniture, and much more. Linda's eight-year-old son, Jeffrey, parted with some of his belongings, including a bicycle, something Herman never dreamed of having. For several nights afterward, Herman slept with his treasured bicycle propped up next to his bed. On several occasions, Christine and Herman have been dinner guests of Linda and her family. Christine was hired as an aide to work in Faith's senior day care center, and she and Herman became members of the church. Somewhere in scripture, we are told that all things are possible through God. How true!

Herman is a very happy boy, and he is enjoying playing soccer on his school team.

When he was baptized, he was informed that, due to his age, it was not necessary for him to have a sponsor at the baptism service. To Linda's surprise, Herman replied that he would like very much to have Linda as his sponsor.

Somewhere in Scripture, we are told that all things are possible through God. How true!

WORDS TO PONDER

"But Mary treasured all these words and pondered them in her heart." (Luke 2:19). A familiar passage that we have heard from the pulpit countless Christmases past! And once again we heard these same words a few weeks ago from Pastor Jost. Did you notice this time, however, how Pastor made a point of drawing our attention to how Mary *pondered* upon the words spoken by the shepherds?

I must admit that I'm not always quick to pick up on what our pastors are saying; but in this instance, it seemed to me that Pastor Jost may have been suggesting that we would do well to make some time in our hurry-up world to do some pondering of our own, especially when it comes to God's word and how we respond to it?

While not all of them are scriptural, there are other words which I believe are also worthy of our pondering, particularly as they relate to our witness to God's love.

These are words of many notable writers, teachers, theologians, philosophers, and world leaders. Here are just a few:

* Live as if Christ died yesterday, rose this morning, and is coming back tomorrow. Martin Luther

*The worst sin toward our fellow creatures is not to hate them, but to be indifferent to them; that's the essence of inhumanity. George Bernard Shaw

*Imagine…if people took their faith to the next level, what might God do? Two thousand years ago, the world was changed by just twelve. It can happen again. Richard Stearns

*Although the world is full of suffering, it is also full of overcoming it. Helen Keller

*If a man shuts his ears to the crying of the poor, he too will cry out and not be answered.

Proverbs 21:13

*We will have to repent in this generation not merely for the vitriolic words of the bad people, but for the appalling silence of the good people. Martin Luther King Jr.

*Never doubt that a small group of thoughtful committed citizens can change the world; indeed, it's the only thing that ever has. Margaret Mead

*To know what is right and not do it is the worst cowardice. Confucius

*The probability that we may fail in the struggle ought not to deter us from the support of a cause we believe to be just. Abraham Lincoln

*And the King will tell them 'Truly I tell you, just as you did it to one of the least of these who are members of my family, you did it to me.' Matthew 25:40

* But the very good news for those of us who want to follow Christ and be part God's plan for the world is that He uses what we have to offer, no matter how unimportant we think it might be. Richard Stearns

These pronouncements were inserted by Richard Stearns at key locations throughout his best-selling book, *The Hole in Our Gospel,* to direct his reader's attention to the plight of the poor and needy in the world and those who have yet to hear about Christ. You may not be in complete agreement with some, but I believe they are all words to ponder.

THE UNVARNISHED TRUTH

L et's not leave Easter just yet. Let's enjoy this grand season as long as we can. Jesus is still with his disciples, teaching them all that his Father had taught him. His Ascension to heaven was only days away. Acts1:3 tells us: "during the forty days after his crucifixion, he appeared to his disciples from time to time, and he proved to them in many ways that he was actually alive." And he talked to them about the Kingdom of God." Pentecost would soon arrive when they would receive his Great Commission to go into the world and preach the Good News. They were all anxious to go and tell the world what they had witnessed; but their Lord must have felt they could benefit from some final outreach instruction.

Wouldn't it be something if we could slip ourselves into the shoes of Jesus' disciples and believe as they who had been with him for three years and seen firsthand what he had said and done? Well, it seems to me that, as Christians, if we believe what is written in the Gospels, we can accomplish just that. Luke writes in the first chapter of his Gospel that he had carefully investigated eyewitness reports of early disciples before writing a "careful account" of his own. Now let's not lose sight of the fact that Luke was a medical doctor and realized the importance of being thorough in his investigations. He had used these skills of observation and analysis in studying the stories about Jesus. The bottom line: We can read Luke's account of the Good News of Jesus' life and knows it is *true*. Now doesn't it follow that we can best armor ourselves with this truth through careful study of his inspired writing and that of Matthew, Mark, John, Paul and others found in the New Testament? Only then can we testify confidently of this truth as did Christ's disciples commissioned to establish the early church.

To be sure many whom Jesus' disciples sought were anxious to hear the Good News; and we are told there are many today who also hunger to know him well. Let us take this to our Lord in prayer so that we can continue to grow God's kingdom.

GREAT JOY

E arly in Matthew's Gospel we begin to learn a lot about Jesus. We learn, for example, how *obedient* he was to his Father. When Jesus went from Galilee to the Jordan River to be baptized by John the Baptist, John protested. He wanted Jesus to baptize *him*. But Jesus replied, that it should be done, "for we must carry out all that God requires. (Mt 3:15)." Here, at the very outset of his ministry, Jesus demonstrates how we are to be obedient to our Father's plan.

Later in Matthew's Gospel (Mt:26), we read again of Christ's perfect reliance upon God's will as he prays in the Garden of Gethsemane, "My Father! If it is possible, let this cup of suffering be taken away from me. Yet I want your will to be done, not mine. Courage! Yes, but also, perfect *obedience*!

Jesus' Baptism was also the scene of another way Christ demonstrated his obedience to God's will. Almost immediately, as his Baptism was consummated, a voice from heaven was heard. "This is my dearly loved Son, who brings me *great joy.*

Many years ago Pastor Stoner addressed this issue in one of his Wednesday morning Bible studies saying, "The reason we are here is to glorify God." Isn't that the way to bring great joy to our God – by glorifying Him?

Matthew has given us a running start on how to be more like Jesus and his disciples.

THIS IS MY STORY

How many times have you heard someone comment on how much we Lutherans love to eat? It's true, isn't it? Sunday morning fellowship hour -- Bible study -- Men's Prayer Breakfast -- Seniors' luncheons -- dinners with our Catholic and Episcopalian brothers and sisters. You name it; we're always eating.

But you know what! I believe there is something else we love to do just as much as eating. We love to sing! And we all have our favorites, don't we? I have several, but the hymn that comes to mind in the context of evangelism is # 390 in the LBW, I Love to Tell the Story.

Pastor Stoner often exhorts us to "tell the story. OUR story -- the Good News and all that Jesus has done for us. He tells us to give it away. But for years I've had the hardest time finding a way to tell my story -- until one morning, while waiting in line at McDonald's for my coffee, I noticed a man about my age standing next to me, who was wearing a cross around his neck.

I always thought of a cross as being jewelry worn by a woman. After first complementing him on how nice it looked, I asked him why he wore it. Did it have some special meaning for him? His brief reply: "How much time do you have?"

By now we both had paid for our coffee, so he pointed to a table by a window where we could sit. For the next half hour he talked, and I listened.

He began by explaining that his cross reminded him of what Jesus had done for him and that his sins had been forgiven by Jesus' sacrifice on the cross, and his resurrection, what he called Jesus' victory over death. But he quickly added, "There's more to it than that." He explained to me that, when he was baptized, God had actually chosen him to be a member of his family. "Think about it," he said. "This makes Jesus my brother. It actually makes me an heir to everything he has, including eternal life with our Father in heaven. It's all in the Bible."

My new friend went on to say that he believed that everything he had in life was given to him by God -- parents who loved him and instilled in him the habit of regular Sunday school and church attendance, a happy childhood, a good education made possible by the sacrifices of his family, his safe-keeping while serving in the Air Force, good jobs and the skills needed to perform – also a lovely wife and three wonderful children, his church, his friends, his comfortable home, and all of his senses and faculties. "Time," he added. "Time to understand how awful my sins were, time to repent and try to live the sort of life Jesus wants me to."

He checked his watch and finished his coffee. I could tell he was beginning to wind down.

Rising from his seat, he said, "I could go on and on, but I think you get my drift."

As we got up to leave, I said, "That's quite a story, but I have one question. What about all of the people who haven't been blessed the way you have? What about them?"

He replied, "If they have Jesus, what more do they really need?"

At the door, I thanked him for telling me his story. He then patted me on the shoulder and said, "Thanks for giving me the chance to tell it."

Actually, this is my story

CHURCH

TELL EVERYONE WHAT HE HAS DONE

Of all that you've been taught over the years, what would you say has had the most profound effect on you? What has had the greatest influence on how you believe you should live your life? For me, I have no doubt, it was something Pastor Stoner imparted to us in one of his Bible studies some years ago when he said, "The reason we are here is to proclaim Jesus."

Now I suppose the Holy Spirit could have used almost anyone to say to me what Pastor Stoner said. In fact, chances are someone already had – perhaps one of our previous pastors. But for some reason, it never registered with me as it did that morning in Bible study.

What's really important, though, is not so much *who* said it as *what* was said. Isn't that so? It kind of brings to mind what we sing in the post Communion canticle every time we worship – "Thank the Lord and sing his praise: tell everyone what he has done."

But when you think about it, how can people tell others about Jesus unless they know him? And how can they *really know* him unless they read about him in the Bible or learn about him in church.

Let us always be thankful for Jesus -- his life, his teachings, his suffering, his death, and his victory over death – all of this for us. We need to share this Good News with others who don't know him.

FIRST TIME VISITORS

L ast winter some of you were kind enough to help us out with visits to our fellow members who had not worshiped with us for some time. And that was good because we need to be sure that everyone feels that they are welcome at St. Paul's ... and that they are missed when we don't see them for a while.

And you know what! That's also true for first-time worshipers at St. Paul's. They need to know that they are welcome, too.

We learned recently of the remarkable success experienced by several congregations in the Greater Milwaukee synod where they learned that ninety per cent of first-time visitors returned to congregations after they were visited promptly – and briefly.

Preferably these visits were made that same Sunday or the following day; and the visits lasted no longer than two or three minutes.

"We do not encourage visiting teams to go into the house" said one of the evangelism chairpersons. "The idea is not to take up a person's time. It's a thank you call, not a "selling-the-church call" she said. "We found that it made visitors feel welcome in a non-threatening way."

We'd like to think that this can work for us, too, and we're going to give it a try. But, again, we need some help. The Milwaukee Synod churches recruited twelve to fourteen to people with a faith and commitment to Christ and a love for their congregation; and they were sent out two-by-two. We'd like to pull together eight to ten such teams. Kathy has already enlisted our Youth Group to do the baking. Now all we need to do is assemble the visiting teams. If you'll give us a hand, we'll give you all the help you need. Just notify pastor or Kathy or Dave Pagenkopf (267-0669), and we'll get back to you quickly to set in motion this simple, effective outreach ministry.

COOKIE PATROL

For several years now, the Cookie Patrol has been an important element of our outreach at St. Paul's. Let me tell you a little about what this team is – and what it is not.

It's made up of a small group of women who bake cookies for delivery to first-time worshipers here at St. Paul's.

It also includes a second body of people who visit these first-time worshipers, taking with them a "welcome bag" containing a Bible, a recent copy of our monthly newsletter *(Chimes)* and other materials describing St. Paul's and the Lutheran Church – plus that small bag of delicious, homemade cookies.

The visit is usually quick and easy (normally two to three minutes) to say that it was nice having them worship with us and to invite them to come again when they can.

It's an opportunity to use a little of the time God has given us to serve him.

It is also a chance to place a Bible in the hands of someone who may not have one. And, finally, it's a moment for us to be who we say we are – *evangelical*.

What our Cookie Patrol is not:

- it's not a hard sell – just a short visit to let people know that they are always welcome at St. Paul's.
- and it is not an attempt to lure anyone away from his or her own church.

During the past year alone sixteen people who were visited became members. But please don't misunderstand. By no means am I saying that they joined because we gave them a Bible and some cookies. Surely the Holy Spirit is working here through the worship leadership of our pastors, our church leaders and, most importantly, through the welcome extended by all of you.

All members are invited to become a part of this fine ministry welcoming first time worshipers.

NEW JERUSALEM

A lbert Schweitzer could have done almost anything with his life. After all, he had earned doctorate degrees in theology, philosophy, medicine, and music. Yet, he found his greatest joy in serving Christ in the jungles of Africa.

I read this in a book I purchased at a recent library book sale. The book: *Lives That Glorify God,* by Amos Lundquist.

Dr. Schweitzer once said of himself that he had been "privileged to do good." I thought to myself: *"what a great man!"* There was no way, I realized, that on my own I could ever be that great.

But I did pray about this. I asked God if he would just help me become as good as I *can* be – if He would show me how to realize my potential as a Christian. What could be better than that?

Let's never forget that God uses ordinary people like us to serve. Jesus tells us in John 14:12 that those who believe in Him will do the works that He did and, in fact, "will do works greater than these..."

So, it is possible to "do good" as Dr. Schweitzer did. Jesus says so. And, when you think about it:

- we do good when we bring our children to church. Pastor Rodger Prois touched on this in his recent sermon when he remarked of Timothy's faith as it was passed on to him by his grandmother, Lois, and by his mother, Eunice. 2 Timothy 1:5;
- we do good when we volunteer to serve at the Trenton Area Soup Kitchen;

- and when we make quilts and shawls and Baptism blankets;
- when we use our carpentry talents and gardening skills to beautify God's house, buildings and grounds;
- and when we invite and welcome.

We could go on and on, couldn't we?

You may recall the story Pastor Prois related that illustrated so clearly how our ELCA World Hunger dollars are used to good effect. The story takes place in a small, run-down town of New Jerusalem, Mexico. It is populated by some one hundred poor and undernourished peasants who were gifted with thirty chickens bought with dollars received from ELCA World Hunger. The abundance of eggs produced by these thirty chickens worked wonders for their diet and enabled them to upgrade their economy by selling their eggs in the market place. They were taught how to use their profits to plant crops that, over the years yielded long needed income and literally saved their lives. All of this from thirty chickens sent to them by ELCA World Hunger.

When we reach out to our neighbors in Mexico and to faraway lands such as Bosnia, Darfur, Namibia, and God only knows where else, we can feel as Dr. Schweitzer felt, that we, too, are "privileged to do good."

Is this outreach? I believe it is. Perhaps, someday, our lives, too, might be defined as *Lives That Glorify God.*

BEYOND MEMBERSHIP

Membership is important. No question! We want everyone to feel welcome at church. Pastor Jost of St. Paul's Lutheran has challenged us to become not just members in Christ's church but *disciples*, as well. He wants us to become more active in Christ's church.

How would you define "disciple?" I looked it up in the dictionary and found it is defined as a *follower* – someone who adheres to another. Now, that could be a lot of people, couldn't it? Mohammed has disciples in the Muslim faith. And there are disciples of Brigham Young among the Mormons. Even Osama bin Laden had his followers, albeit mislead.

I am reminded of something I recently read about Albert Schweitzer, the great physician and theologian, who ministered to the tribes in Africa during the early twentieth century. The good doctor noted that people are often prone to say, "Oh, I would like to do some good in the world, but with so many responsibilities at home and in business, my nose is always to the grindstone." Or, "I am sunk in my own petty affairs, and there is no chance for my life to mean anything." But he went on to say that, "any human being can assert his personality by seizing every opportunity for spiritual activity."

Now you may be thinking: *I come to church every week. Isn't that being spiritually active?* And, of course, it is. But pastor believes that we are capable of more. He would like see more of us being spiritually active, not just on Saturday night or Sunday morning, but on at least one additional day during the week. I think he would like to see us reassessing our priorities to make this happen.

And you know what? There are many ways of becoming more active here at St. Paul's. Take for example, teaching Sunday School or helping out with Vacation Bible School, Altar Guild, singing with the choir, maintaining the buildings and grounds; helping assimilate new members, flower delivery to shut-ins.

After contemplating all of the spiritual gifts you have received from God, I'll just bet you can find a place where they can be put to good use. Why not talk it over with the pastor? I'm certain he could help.

FROM ORDINARY TO EXTRAORDINARY

I n one of his sermons Pastor Stoner told us a story about a man by the name of Mack McMann. He was the guy out in California who tried to convince a friend of his to go with him to a revival meeting. But his friend wasn't that interested and declined the invitation. Then Mack remembered that his friend had a passion for trucks and he thought - if I offer to let him drive my truck to the revival meeting, maybe he'll go along with me. Well, sure enough, that did the trick. You probably know the rest of the story. As it turns out, Mack's friend was a young man by the name of Billy Graham – a man who would go on to travel the globe bringing millions to Christ.

Some of you may recall the name of Billy Sunday, an evangelist who was to the first half of the twentieth century what Billy Graham was to the second half. In one of his sermons Sunday told a similar story of another gentleman who went into a shoe store in Boston and found a young fellow selling shoes and boots. While in the store, they became somewhat acquainted and, as was his practice, the older man soon introduced the salesman to Jesus Christ and eventually won him over to Christ. The name of the young salesman was Dwight L Moody, a man who during the mid-nineteenth century went on to become one of America's greatest evangelists. Over 100 million people were influenced by his ministry – and all of this without the benefit of radio or television.

So, while Moody's name became well-known throughout this country and many parts of the world, hardly anyone knows the name of the man who won Moody for Christ.

Billy Sunday closes the story by revealing the man's name simply as Kimball, an ordinary man whom God used to win Moody. But it was Moody who went on to win the multitude.

We're all pretty ordinary people much like Mack McCann and the shoe customer named Kimble. And not too unlike another ordinary person named Andrew who went to his brother, Peter, and brought him to Jesus. Perhaps someday God will use us in a similar fashion. Maybe he already has.

A DECISION FOR CHRIST

F ollowing his June, 1955 graduation from Rutgers University
David Mangiante accepted a Sales position with the J.P.
Stevens Company, a prominent textile manufacturer with offices
at Broadway and 41st Street, New York City. He worked primarily
as an Inside Salesman of Stevens cloths to customers and
manufacturer's representatives. Additionally he was responsible
for expediting deliveries of fall and winter merchandise to Stevens'
customers. Periodically he found it helpful to travel to some of
the company's textile mills in New England to familiarize himself
with the milling processes and to maintain good rapport with the
mill personnel. Dave enjoyed his work and looked forward to a
long future with the company.

His business trips typically took him north on the Merritt
Parkway into Connecticut, Massachusetts, and New Hampshire.
Generally his nights were spent in homes having rooms for rent
signs on the front lawns.

As a young man in the early 50's, Dave worshiped at Bethany
Lutheran Church in North Bergen, N.J. where he also served

on church council. Little did he realize that he was about to experience a sudden transformation in his career plans and, indeed, in his whole life. For it was at this time that all Lutheran churches of the ELCA New Jersey Synod were notified of the need for volunteer teachers of youngsters scheduled to attend a summer youth assembly/gathering at Camp Beisler (now called Camp Crossroads)

N.J. Dave's strong educational background in Science uniquely satisfied the need for a teacher of this subject, and he became Bethany's volunteer.

When he arrived at Beisler, he learned that he would be sharing living quarters with seven others—all of them pastors. To his surprise Dave was quite taken by his new friends, finding them to be rather ordinary guys possessing strong Christian attitudes toward life and the church. By summer's end Dave found himself seriously questioning whether his future was in textiles or perhaps in the Lord's service as a Lutheran minister.

So he decided to take a week of his vacation and travel by himself. Dave thought this might give him the privacy he needed to consider his options: remain with J.P. Stevens or enroll in the fall semester at the Philadelphia Seminary.

While traveling that week of decision, Dave used his Bible for his daily devotions. One evening while in his room, his RSV Bible fell open to Romans 10:14, and he began to read the words of St. Paul: "But how are men to call upon him in whom they have not believed? And how are they to believe in him of whom they have never heard? And how are they to hear without a preacher? And how can men preach unless they are sent….? When Dave set his Bible aside that night, his decision was made. Three years later at age 28 he completed his seminary studies and accepted his first call: Christ Lutheran Church in Bridgeton, New Jersey

Retirement followed 35 years later – five at Christ Lutheran,

Bridgeton, N.J., seven at Nativity Lutheran, East Brunswick, N.J. and the final 23 years caring for his flock here at St. Paul's.

Actually it might be more accurate to say that he *semi*-retired – because he's still at it. St. Michaels in Moorestown enjoyed his year and one-half as their Interim Pastor; and he still receives calls almost every week from Synod office asking him to accept Supply Pastor assignments at churches as far north as Washington Township N.J. and to Cape May and Millville to the South. That spans some fifty-five years since he preached his first sermon as Pastor at Bridgeton.

On our way home from the golf course recently I asked him why. "Why do you still do it?" You're supposed to be retired!." His reply: "because I enjoy it --and they need it."

Imagine, if you can, how many souls have been touched by this man over the past fifty-five years of his service to the Lord. Thanks be to God, David Mangiante was inspired by Paul's appeal as recorded in the 10th chapter of Romans. And he has spent a lifetime responding to Jesus' command to "go and make disciples….(Mt.28:19) I think that makes for a beautiful outreach story. I hope you agree.

AN ALTERNATIVE GIFT

S everal years ago, the plight of the hungry in the world was brought into sharp focus in *The Lutheran*. The enormity of this problem staggers the imagination. Almost 800,000,000 of the world's population are undernourished.

We here at St. Paul's have not been oblivious to this dire need. Every year our Social Ministry team prepares for us a delicious World Hunger breakfast. In June alone, World Hunger received almost $1,400 from our breakfast contributions and Thrivent's match. Many of our members, I'm sure, use the World Hunger envelope that comes every month with our *Chimes* newsletter. That's terrific! But is it enough? Remember: almost 800,000,000 people.

It makes one wonder why God blesses us with so much while so many millions go hungry. A Bible passage (John 9: 1-4) comes to mind, which Pastor Stoner discussed with us during a gathering of our Wednesday morning study group. When Jesus' disciples asked him why this man was born blind, He answered, "… so that God's works may be revealed to him." Could it be that God wants us to see how we might respond to this most desperate need of the hungry?

Pastor Jost and I asked our Men's Prayer Breakfast group how we here at St. Paul's might be able to make a difference. As you might expect, pastor came up with an idea. "It won't be long "he said, "before the stores will be stuffing our mail boxes with catalogs and sales brochures announcing their holiday shopping bargains. Maybe we could beat them to the punch and, at the same time, help everyone here get a jump on the stores by giving them some alternative gift ideas for Christmas."

How does this sound? When our family members or friends ask us what we would like for Christmas, why not just ask them to write a check and send it to ELCA World Hunger Appeal instead of spending a lot of money for that tie or bottle of perfume that we really don't need.

Kathryn Sime, Director of ELCA World Hunger and Disaster Appeal at that time, was kind enough to give us some suggestions of how we might help. For example:

Your gift of $30.00 would:

– provide one month of care for an abandoned street child; or
– buy chickens in Kenya - or a pig in Haiti.

Your gift of $20.00 would:

– help stock and build a fish farm in Tanzania.

Your gift of $10 – 15.00 would buy a pair of rabbits in Peru or Uganda or help start a duck-raising business in Cambodia.

Your gift of $1.00 would feed and care for a hungry child for one day.

Good shopping!

THE BETHEL BIBLE SERIES

S oon after accepting his call to ministry at St. Paul's Evangelical Lutheran Church in Hainesport, New Jersey, Pastor David Mangiante introduced a study designed to remind people of the basic principles that can be found in the Bible – one such principle being that we are all blessed by God so that we can be a blessing to others.

The Bethel Bible Series is an intensive study of the Bible. Our new pastor then used this study for two years to teach ten members of the congregation what they should know about the Bible and our Christian faith. After two years of intensive study, these ten were fully equipped to teach the other members of the congregation for another four years. Some of you fine folks are still with us some forty- five years later. It was during that four year period that the congregation adopted as our church motto: *Blessed to be a blessing,* - the way we try to live our lives and minister to others around the world.

Pastor has said that he considers this Bethel Bible Series Study to be the high point of his 25 year ministry here at St. Paul's

This motto is artfully represented by a stained glass window which Pastor M. had installed in our Sanctuary and can be seen high overhead as you exit the Nave to enter the Narthex. As you look up at that window, you will observe a beam of light coming from on high, representing God's blessings which are being directed toward a tear drop of water. This drop of water symbolizes the Church of God. That's us! We, in turn, acting as a prism of sorts, reflect God's beam of light into a myriad of wonderful blessings being bestowed upon people worldwide.

Pastor defines these as God's gifts to us of time, talents, and treasures which we are to share with others in need.

Abudanza is a term Pastor Jost once used to describe the abundance of blessings which God has lavished upon us. And just what exactly might these blessings be?

How about his gift of love, his *unconditional* love for us? And also his grace, his mercy, his everlasting presence. We could go on and on, couldn't we?

We are often reminded that we are to share our blessings with others and that, when we do, we are not just serving them, but God as well...

Pastor Mangiante, please accept our heartfelt thanks for this beautiful stained glass window reminding us of God's countless blessings.

THE CHALLENGE OF DISCIPLESHIP

B y now, you will have read in the Annual Report the challenging goals that Pastor Jost has entrusted to the Evangelism Team for the year ahead. Challenging, yes; but pastor also believes they are attainable. But we're going to need your help.

In years past our primary concern has been one of membership – i.e., inviting people to come to church where they can hear and learn about Jesus. How often have you heard our pastors repeat to us the words Jesus spoke to his disciples "Come and see!"

Membership is important. No question! We want everyone to feel welcome at St. Paul's. But this year Pastor Jost is challenging us to become more active in Christ's church -- not just members, but *disciples*, as well.

How would you define "disciple?" I looked it up in the dictionary and found that it is defined as a *follower* – someone who adheres to another. Now that could be a lot of people, couldn't? Mohammed has disciples in the Muslim faith. And there are disciples of Brigham Young among the Mormons. Even Osama bin Laden had his followers, albeit mislead.

I am reminded of something that I read about Albert Schweitzer, the great physician and theologian who ministered to the tribes in Africa during the early twentieth century. The good doctor noted that people are often prone to say, "Oh, I would like to do some good in the world; but with so many responsibilities at home and in business, my nose is always to the grindstone. I am sunk in my own petty affairs, and there is no chance for my life to mean anything." But he went on to say that "any human being can assert his personality by seizing every opportunity for spiritual activity."

Now you may be thinking to yourself – I come to church every week. Isn't that being spiritually active? And, of course, it is. But pastor believes that we are capable of more. He would like to see more of us being spiritually active not just on Saturday night or Sunday morning, but on at least one additional day during the week. I think that he would like to see us reassessing our priorities to make this happen.

And you know what? There are many ways of becoming more active here at St. Paul's. Take, for example, teaching Sunday School, or helping out with Vacation Bible School; Altar Guild; singing with one of the choirs; maintaining our buildings and grounds; helping assimilate new members, flower delivery to shut-ins.

And there are still more outlets for becoming more involved. If you would like to learn how to become a more faithful disciple of Jesus, please give this your prayerful consideration and see if there isn't some way of arranging your busy schedule. If you would like to reach that next level of discipleship, just "come and see" what it's all about.

GOD'S PEOPLE

Have you ever stopped to think about how fortunate we are to be members of Christ's church?

If you give it some thought, I'm sure you can come up with several reasons. As for me, I feel mostly blessed because, when I'm here at my church, I know I am with God's people. That's not to say that we alone are God's people, because we know that God loves everyone. But it's really a neat feeling when I'm with all of my friends at St. Paul's. Think about it!

* When we are at worship, we are with God's people.
* When we are at Bible study, we are with God's people.
* When choir members convene for practice, they are with God's people.

* We are with God's people when we meet for Men's Prayer Breakfast, just as the ladies are when they are at one of their woman's circle gatherings.
* When the Needle and Thread ladies gather on Wednesday mornings, they are with God's people.
* Every time you walk into the church office, you are with God's people.

We could go on and on. Nicky Gumbel, the man who was so instrumental in the design and growth of the ALPHA course, says it well in his book, *Questions of life*.

A few of his comments: "Let us not give up meeting together, as so many are in the habit of doing, but let us encourage one another…." – "It (the church) is a place where lasting friendships can be made." – "The church is made up of people who belong to God, bound together in love as a family, representing Christ to the world …." – "A Christian out of fellowship is like a coal out of the fire."

You may be asking yourself what all of this has to do with Evangelism. Try to look at it this way: God says we must love him with all we've got, and our neighbors also. So, if we really *do* love our neighbors (friends and family also), why would we *not* want to share with them the joy and fellowship that is ours when we are with God's people?

There are many, we are told, who are just waiting to be invited by us.

ABUDANZA

Pastor Jost once used this term in a sermon to describe the *abundance* of blessings we enjoy here at St. Paul's. And it's true, isn't it?

Our recent congregational meeting brought this home to me big time. Think of it! Our Christian education program is growing. Our social ministry to the community manifests itself in so many ways. Our stewardship giving is up. And the overall management of our church affairs appears to be in good hands -- witness the refinancing of our church mortgage to take advantage of a lower fixed interest rate, saving us money. Consider how many other churches struggle to minister on the scale we do.

Most impressive, in my view, is our Youth Program and how it's thriving. This bodes well for St. Paul's in the years ahead, especially from an evangelism perspective.

Inviting seems to come so naturally to some of our youth. Let me cite you a couple of examples.

A few weeks ago, I met a young girl in the narthex by the name of Dana. She had come to worship at the invitation of her friends, Meghan and Christine, daughters of Elaine Lutz. The three girls have also been attending St. Paul's H.O.T. (Here on Thursdays) youth meetings.

I asked Dana if she would sign our guest register. And a few days later, I followed up with a Cookie Patrol welcome visit to her home. She was in school, but her father (a very nice man) answered the door and told me how much Dana was enjoying the Thursday nights with our H.O.T group. I learned later that

Meghan and Christine had also invited others of their friends to H.O.T. and also to worship on Sunday mornings.

Debbie Eagle's daughter, Amanda, has been doing the same thing. Her good friend, Nicky, has been attending worship services as well the H.O.T. meetings with Amanda. There are several others of our youngsters, I am sure, who are also inviting just as Meghan and Christine and Amanda have been doing.

We are indeed most richly blessed, and in many, many ways it seems we are blessed to be a blessing to others.

PENTECOST SET TO MUSIC

S ome fifty days after Passover, a group of believers became conscious of a strong presence while engaged in silent prayer. Peter was among them and said that it must be the coming of the Spirit of Truth that Jesus had promised. It was that day that Peter preached his now-famous sermon, and some 3,000 souls were baptized. The Spirit of Truth dwelled in their hearts. The Christian Church was born; and we celebrate this historic event every year on Pentecost Sunday. And what a celebration it is!

This year Marge Swartz and her Cherub Choir really got us into the Pentecost spirit with their lively rendition of two spirited songs: the first being *Everybody Ought to Know*. I invite you to sing along with me. We'll start with the refrain

> *"Everybody ought to know who Jesus is.*
> *He's my Savior and he loves me, caring for me every day.*
> *He will never, never leave me; he will guide me all the way. Everybody ought to know who Jesus is.*
> *He's my guide and he will lead me over any path I go*
> *He will always go before me; he's the one you ought to know Everybody ought to know who Jesus is."*

What a jolly time these kids have singing! What energy and enthusiasm! And what a blessing they are!

Later in the service they delighted us with an encore, telling us in song what we must do once we get to know this Jesus. It's a sending song: *Go, We Gotta Go* - and Jesus goes with us.

> *"Go, go, go, go, go, -____We gotta go Take the*
> *love of Jesus, take it with you every day.*
> *Take the love of Jesus and then give, give it away.*
> *Take the hope of Jesus; take it with you every day.*
> *Take the hope of Jesus, and then give, give it away.*
> *Take the peace of Jesus with you every day*
> *Take the peace of Jesus, and then give, give it*
> *away.*

The two songs kind of go together, don't they? Kind of like sugar and spice go together, and bacon and eggs. And how many of you remember that all-time great hit of Frank Sinatra's a couple of generations back? : *Love and marriage, love and marriage, go together like a horse and carriage ...*

"Oh! Sorry about that! I got a little carried away".

Have you noticed how our children's choirs are being given star billing in some of our Pentecost worship services? I love it. Perhaps it has something to do with the fact that our pastor studied and then taught music for ten years before entering seminary. How often have we heard him offer his "thanks upon thanks" for this or for that? Maybe we should offer him our "thanks upon thanks" for assembling such a fine musical staff over the years. We are, indeed, blessed to have so many fine musicians willing and able to give of their time and talents to praise and glorify our Lord.

THE TORN CURTAIN

" Then Jesus gave a loud cry and breathed his last. And the curtain of the temple was torn in two."

The torn curtain symbolism used here by the writer of this second gospel tells us, I believe, that Jesus' death opened a *way* for us to have access to God. Without his sacrifice for us on the cross we would be separated from God forever. His sacrifice makes it possible for us to be in our Father's presence. Would this be your understanding also? If so, we must now be alert for opportunities to bring this good news to others who are unaware of what Christ has done for us.

During a recent Tuesday morning Bible class session Pastor Johnson brought out this truth for us again with his reading from Colossians 2: 20-22: "…. And through him -- (ie., Christ)-- God *reconciled* everything to himself. He made peace with everything in heaven and on earth by means of Christ's blood on the cross. This includes all of us who were once away from God.

We had been his enemies, separated from him by our evil thoughts and actions. But now he has *reconciled* us to himself through the death of Christ. As a result he has brought us into his own presence.

As he often does, Pastor Johnson concluded his reading with a profound "Wow! Is that powerful, or what!" – referring not to his reading, of course, but rather to Scripture itself.

Matthew Henry also picked up on this in his Concise Commentary, noting that "It pleased God to reconcile fallen man to himself by the sacrifice and death of Christ in our nature …."

It is that word "reconciled", used in both readings that caught my attention. I thought I understood its meaning, but to be sure, I looked it up in my dictionary; and this is what I found: "to make good again – to repair – to restore to communion in the church, our sins forgiven."

Reconciled! I like that word. More good news for all of us.

WHAT A GUY!

I am beginning to record my thoughts about this man a full month before the article is due in the church office for the June issue of Chimes. Why? Because I knew it was going to take some time to do justice to such a gentleman as Harold Gray.

As I returned Max Lucado's book, *Just like Jesus*, to my book shelf, I wondered if I knew anyone who might deserve such high praise. After considerable thought, Harold Gray came to mind. Fortunately, my article wasn't due in the church office for a few weeks; and that was good, because I knew it would take some time to gather my thoughts together in order to do justice to such a fine gentleman as Harold.

Lucado says it so nicely in his book: God loves us just as we are. After all, we are all made in his image. The more I thought about it, Harold Gray was clearly one of the most Christ-like persons I knew. In Harold's case, I doubt God would have to make many changes – just a tweak here and a tweak there, and he would have a really fine finished product, bearing a very close resemblance to his Master.

I don't know whether Harold liked to fish, but had he lived in Galilee during biblical times, there's a pretty good chance Jesus might have looked him up and asked him to "Follow me, and I will make you a fisher of men." I feel certain that, just like Peter and Andrew, Jesus' first disciples, Harold would have dropped everything and done just as he was told.

How can I be so sure? Harold was a devout, church-going man who I had the privilege of knowing for over fifty years. He was a loving person and a lovable person. He was a moral person, a Christian in every sense of the word. Never, ever did I hear an unkind word cross his lips. That's probably how he came to be what he was – humble, upright, and so very good. In short, he had all the qualities Jesus would seek in a disciple.

As I think back, it was one week to the day that I had a chance to be with him before he died. My wife Laura. had just made a pot of homemade vegetable soup, which I left in his refrigerator.

After some forty-five minutes, I could tell he was getting tired. Perhaps I had overstayed my welcome. As I drove home, I realized what a privilege it was to have been with him. Curiously, I felt a kind of pleasure when I learned that I had at least one thing in common with him. You see, we talked briefly about prayer. And, to my surprise, one of our prayers we still recited at day's end was one we had both learned as a child.

> Now I lay me down to sleep;
> I pray Thee, Lord, my soul to keep. If I should
> die before I wake,
> I pray Thee, Lord, my soul to take. If I should live
> for other days,
> I pray Thee, Lord, to guide my ways. Amen.

We laughed about this – the fact that we had both enjoyed this simple prayer learned so very long ago. Whether we died or lived; either way would be just fine, as long as we were with our Lord.

Harold Gray had put Christ first in his life - a life ending just shy of his ninety–seventh birthday. – a life-long member of St. Paul's, regular worship, and service to his Lord as Sunday School Superintendent, – Men's Prayer Breakfast – Friday Fellows – loving husband, father and grandfather. And always smiling!

What a guy!

PEOPLE WE DON'T EVEN KNOW

The shocking news of an earthquake in Haiti a few years ago left people heartsick around the world. Hundreds of thousands of people losing families, homes, businesses, and hope.

During the ensuing weeks the news media brought us heroic stories of people saved, orphans adopted, and needs being met with love and prayer and care.

What seems most remarkable to me about all of this is the unconditional love exhibited by so many people for others they don't even know. This is especially true of Americans, I believe. We are good at responding. And we do it first, and with the most. Our Lord must be pleased.

And it's also true of Christ's church here on Marne Highway, Hainesport, N.J. Our Lord must be pleased with our outreach of love to our neighbors in Bosnia, New Orleans, and the more than 800 million undernourished around the world. Again, these are people we don't even know. And so it has been with the time and talents shared so lovingly by our Social Ministry team, our lady quilters, our shawl sharers, and all who are feeding the hungry with their offerings to ELCA World Hunger and World Vision.

As grand as our outreach ministries have been here at St. Paul's, it's always nice to hear stories of individuals who are acting in tangible ways, and doing it on their own. I learned of such a story recently that I believe is worth telling. It's Glenn McMahon's story; but I didn't hear it from him.

It seems that Glenn's commute to his office in Chesterfield sometimes takes him through New Hanover Township and past the Rose of Sharon Lutheran Church in Wrightstown. On his way home one evening, Glenn's attention was drawn to a church sign announcing the closing of the food bank at Rose of Sharon Lutheran. The sign stated in bold block letters: PANTRY CLOSING – NO MORE FOOD – PLEASE HELP.

This bothered Glenn, so much so that he detoured to a nearby Shop Rite food store and purchased several bags of groceries; and he returned them to the church.

When he arrived home, he immediately phoned some friends to ask for help. He contacted the local newspaper, and they sent a reporter to the church. A few days later an article appeared in the paper appealing to the generosity of the people and urging them to bring what they could to help this worthy cause.

Sure enough, a few days later, another message appeared on the church sign: PANTRY OPEN – THANK YOU! – THANK YOU! – THANK YOU!

No matter what the need, whether it is world-wide, national, or local; no matter from whom the response is made; when people do for others, and it's done in love, we boldly witness our faith as Christians to others. Our light shines, and we bring glory to our Father in heaven.

> *if you help the poor, you are lending to the*
> *Lord -- and he will repay you.*
> *Proverbs 19:17*

BECAUSE YOU INVITED US

I can't remember ever being disappointed with any of the workshops I have attended at the Conference of Congregational Ministries, particularly with any session headed up by Rev. Bruce Ewan, assistant to the bishop. When I learned that he was to lead a workshop on *Inviting*, I enrolled right away.

After all participants settled into their classroom seats, Rev. Ewan opened the session by inviting each of us to pair off and exchange any experiences we had with inviting people to church. Well, I was all cocked and ready to go with this; and right away I told my partner – I think her name was Sonya – about all the friends and relatives we had invited to our Christmas Eve services. I told her how St. Paul's parishioners had distributed more than one hundred cassettes of *The Sounds of Christmas* to those they had invited to church. And then I told her that, on the day after Christmas, our Cookie Patrol had set a new Guinness Book of World Records with twenty-six visits to persons who worshiped at St. Paul's for the first time on Christmas Eve. I mean I was pretty pumped up about this.

Sonya listened patiently until I wound down, and then she told me of an experience she had at her church – some church up in north Jersey. I forget where exactly. And you know what? Her story was just as good as mine – maybe better.

It seems that Sonya had a friend – let's call her Ruth – and Ruth wanted to get married. But she was having a hard time finding a church that would marry her. You see, she was betrothed to a gentleman who was Catholic – and he was also divorced.

Apparently, he either couldn't or didn't wish to be wed in a Catholic church.

But that's not the end of the story. Soon after, as Sonya was sitting in the front pew with her family on a Sunday morning when Ruth and her brand new husband, home from their honeymoon, squeezed in next to them. As they were heading up the aisle after the service, Sonya told Ruth and her husband how happy she was they had decided to come back to church. And Ruth replied "We are, too. In fact, we've decided to join the church. And then it will be our church, and it's because you invited us."

I thought this was kind of a neat story. It goes to show that there are all kinds of opportunities to invite people to church. And what could be more satisfying than to know it was your invitation that allowed this to happen?

AND YOU WERE PART OF IT

D id you know that you recently helped save the life of a Liberian baby boy very sick with malaria? Well, you did; and here's the story.

A young, single mother living in a rural Liberian community knew her baby was sick when he refused to eat. Because immediate medical attention was not an option, she and her child set out that morning on a long journey through the brush to reach a hospital.

After carrying her child for hours, the woman came upon a river that required a ferry to get across. It was almost midday before she made it to the other side, and by then her baby had a fever. Another full day of walking brought her to a road. There she got a ride in the back of a pick-up, enduring two hours on a dusty road before finally reaching her destination.

Phebe Hospital in Banga County, Liberia, took the woman in, according to Dr. Garfee T. Williams, the hospital's medical director. The baby was malnourished, and the doctor was not sure the baby would live. But, he said there was a chance because of the faith of people who share their resources. (That's you).

The ELCA's involvement at Phebe Hospital … provides medical treatment when necessary for people like this mother and her baby, at little or no cost to them.

Gifts to the ELCA World Hunger Appeal, administered through the ELCA Global Mission unit, rebuilt Phebe Hospital twice during turbulent war years (1990-2006) and continue to help fight malaria and other diseases of poverty by helping communities access health care, learn about nutrition, improve agricultural techniques, and much more.

For more information on the work of the ELCA in Liberia go to: Walking with the Lutheran Church in Liberia: http//www. elca.org/liberia. Gifts to support this ministry - checks made out to ELCA World Hunger Appeal - may be sent through your congregation or directly to: ELCA World Hunger Appeal. P.O. Box 71764, Chicago IL 60694-1764. Contributions may be made on line at http.www.org/goodgifts.

Now you may be wondering just how you played a part in this child's victory over malaria.

Read on!

When you drop your envelope into the offering plate or contribute through *Simply Giving*, three per cent of what you give goes directly to ELCA World Hunger Appeal. Let's do the math. If you give an average of $20 per week, 3 percent (sixty cents) goes to ELCA World Hunger.

Doesn't sound like much, does it? But when you do that for 52 weeks, it adds up to $31.20.

Not bad! And, when an average of 200 worshipers doing the same thing, we're up to $6,240 for the year. Not all of that went to Phebe Hospital, of course; but you can be certain that some of it did. And you were part of it!!

Ordinarily I try to write something more original each month and, of course, this story did not originate with me. I read it in an issue of *Seeds for the* Parish, an ELCA publication, and it seemed too good to pass up. You might make the case that a story that speaks of sharing our treasures is not so much an evangelism story as it is of stewardship, and I would agree. But can't it be both? This is a story about reaching out. Wasn't it Jesus who once said to the righteous …"Truly I tell you, just as you have done it to one of the least of these who are members of my family, you did it to me." Mt. 25:40

SMART CHOICES

These few lines may read more like something coming from a Christian Education Committee than from an Evangelism Team, but that's okay. As you read on, I believe you'll see how there can be some overlap between these two ministries.

I've had the pleasure of sitting with my church's Adult Education group that meets in the library on Sunday mornings between worship services. Those people attending have some really intriguing discussions. For instance, the group has been talking about SMART CHOICES: helping us examine how we might live a life that is faithful to Christian principles.

A couple of weeks were devoted to a discussion of Mission Statements – not just the kind we've adopted for our St. Paul's congregation; but rather a *personal* Mission Statement – that is, a kind of spiritual guideline one might adopt as one's own.

When asked, one person remarked she was attempting to keep foremost in her mind that "God is Love." She tried to live her life in response to the gift of God's love for her. Another person stated he was trying to celebrate the diversity of others. And yet another said he would like to be guided by asking himself "What would Jesus do or say in any given situation?"

I suggested the post-communion canticle found on page 92 of the Lutheran Book of Worship might serve as a fine personal mission statement: "Thank the Lord and sing his praise; tell everyone what he has done ..." Some of the beautiful hymns we sing remind us of what it is to be evangelical – "Lift High the Cross, the Love of Christ Proclaim" or "I Love to Tell the Story."

Perhaps in the future, it might be fun to explore just how we might "tell the story" of Jesus and what he has done for us. After all, isn't that why we're here?

BAPTISM- REBIRTH AS A CHILD OF GOD

I t seems it has taken me forever to become fully alive to all of the good news in the Bible, which is ours to revel in. This really struck home as I followed along in the Baptism service of Braydon Salzwedel, great- grandson of Bill and Marge Gardner.

Pastor directed us to the page where we read, "In Baptism our gracious heavenly Father *frees us from sin and death* by joining us to the death and resurrection of our Lord Jesus Christ." Now that's really Good News, isn't it? But there's more!

We are then told that "by water and the Spirit we are *reborn as children of God* and made members of the church, the body of Christ."

We have heard these loving words countless times, but only recently have they really begun to register with me. Just imagine! We are all God's children. Does it get any better than that?

Indeed! We are reminded that "we are *living with Christ* and in the communion of saints." That's pretty good company.

Then we recite the Apostles' Creed: "On the third day *he arose again*." There's no arguing that this is the greatest event in the history of the world.

As the pastor and family leave the baptismal font, Braydon hears that he has been *sealed by the Holy Spirit and marked with the cross of Christ forever*. How neat is that?

After Braydon's parents and sponsors promise to help him grow as a Christian, we hear those familiar words: "Let your light so shine before others that they may see your good works and glorify your Father in heaven".

Certainly, it will be some time before Braydon understands

what happened to him on that joyous day; but knowing the Gardners as I do, there will come a day when Braydon most assuredly will know and understand he has been, and always will be, a child of God.

Finally, this neat little guy is introduced to all of us in the congregation, and he is invited to join us in *bearing God's creative and redeeming word to all the world"*.

This is where we come in, isn't it? Braydon has just been invited to join us in telling the story of Jesus and what He has done.

Pastor Jost likes to remind us that baptism is not something any of us choose; but that God has chosen us. Have you ever wondered why?

God only knows; but for some reason He loves us. And He loves little Braydon, too. And that is Good News.

THAT'S WHAT I WANT FOR MY CHILD

For me, one of the highlights of Sunday morning worship is the children's sermons delivered by our Associate Pastor, Kathy Knodt. And that's not meant to be a "knock" on Pastor's Jost's sermons. But seeing that flock of bright, young faces come forward on his invitation is like a breath of spring. And with arms stretched high, some of them just can't wait to show everyone they know the answers to Kathy's questions.

From my vantage point in the choir, it's almost as much fun watching the expressions on the faces of adults in the congregation as they strain to see what's going on up front.

Oh, one or two of the little ones may decide to roam around the altar or do some gymnastics on the Communion rail – and that's not so good. But the really important thing is that *they are all in church* – right under the cross and locked into Kathy's story of Jesus and his love and care for all of them.

And just why *are* they there? Could it be that their parents love them enough to make certain they are there?

And that's being evangelical, too, isn't it? These parents are witnessing to their children. They are instilling in them the good Christian habit of attending church on Sunday mornings. Who knows? Maybe one or two of these kids will invite a friend to Vacation Bible School or to Sunday school. Perhaps, the parents or sponsors of a child being baptized will notice how much our youngsters delight in these children's sermons – or how much they enjoy singing in the Cherub or Chapel choirs. And they may decide then and there "That's what I want for my child."

Of course, it's always possible that, as they grow older, one or two of these kids will stray from the church. But with the solid Christian foundation they are getting from their parents early on, chances are there won't be too many wanderers, and even if there are, someday they'll be back.

STILL REAL! STILL RELEVANT!

S till Real. Still Relevant! Sound familiar! It should!

It was this very theme that we adopted one year ago to remind us that the church and Jesus Christ are still real and still relevant.

We had remarkable success with this program last year; and Pastor Stoner has now asked us to embrace this same theme again this year.

What we plan is an even more focused evangelism effort to bring the Good News of Jesus Christ to others in our family and community.

During the weeks ahead leading up to Christmas you will all be afforded special opportunities to be an evangelical church.

* You will have opportunities to invite people to be among us for worship, for Sunday School, for Bible study, for Wednesday Night Advent services and for other special events being planned.
* You will be encouraged to meditate upon persons you would like to invite.
* You will see publicity promoting the Still Real, Still Relevant theme
* You will be asked to pray for persons you know who have special needs.
* Bulletin inserts will be available to you with suggestions that you may find useful as you extend your invitations.
* You will hear Temple Talks highlighting the Still Real, Still Relevant theme.

* You will be given audio cassette tapes to distribute as you invite others to join us.
* And you will be asked to pray for all of us who will be inviting and for those. whom we invite.

The gospel writers remind us of Jesus' command to love one another. And Pastor Stoner takes this one step further in our Bible study: if we are able to love others as Jesus commands, why would we not want to share this Good News with them?

A MESSAGE FROM THE BISHOP

Pastor Jost once showed me an e-mail he received from then-presiding Bishop Mark Hanson. The bishop noted that, at a recent synod assembly, the question was asked, "What should be the priorities of the ELCA?" The overwhelming response was "evangelism and outreach." Up to that time, I had never given much thought to the term, *evangelism*, only that, to me, at least, it was some kind of religious dogma, or doctrine, which was of little interest to me.

But this quickly changed as I read some of Bishop Hanson's thoughts on the subject.

- Evangelism is the Good News of Jesus Christ. It is the vocation of all the baptized.
- It is proclaiming and inviting.
- It is the gracious word spoken by forgiven sinners....proclaiming the crucified and risen Christ.
- It is about sharing Jesus, not promoting the Church. It is an invitation, not a confrontation. In ordinary life, Christians' witness is at the heart of evangelism.

Over the years, evangelism has come to mean a great deal more to me. It has led me to understand what Jesus intends for us with his Great Commission found in the twenty-eighth chapter of Matthew's Gospel (v.v. 19-20); "to go and make disciples....and to teach them to obey all of his commands...."

245

Knowing of my growing interest in this subject, my daughter, Linda, showed me a booklet she received through her church. It was written for Lutheran Hour Ministries by Andrew T. Fitzgerald. His title: *The Secret of Successful Evangelism*. Like Bishop Hanson's message, this booklet offered concepts on evangelism, some of which were new to me, and may be of interest to you.

Healthy evangelism comes from gratitude, not obligation. The secret is in *being*, not *doing*. The starting point should be truly understanding what the Gospel is, and what it means to us.

Our obligations are met by God's grace through Jesus.

We don't have to worry or fret about earning our way into heaven. We don't have to be evangelists to be saved.

We don't have to feel obligated to share the Gospel. It's a mistake to feel guilty – or to force Jesus into every conversation we have with unbelievers.

Guilt makes evangelism a burden, not a blessing. It should just be a natural part of our lifestyle.

The Holy Spirit places us in the right place, at the right time, and with the right words. We do not go alone. He goes with us, and empowers us.

As I read over what I have written here, it occurs to me once again, that I should acknowledge the obvious - that all of what I have written does not originate with me. And I realize, also, that a lot of this is not as new to you as it is to me. But I believe that repetition can sometimes be beneficial. Isn't that how we learned, as youngsters in school, our multiplication tables, and in church, our Lord's Prayer, the Apostles' Creed, and His ten commandments?

Food for thought.

JUST LIKE JESUS

M any churches, like St. Paul's, have ongoing book study groups. Perhaps you are participating in one right now. I would like to heartily recommend for your study a book I recently read which I consider extraordinary. Max Lucado is the author. Its title: *A Heart like Jesus. He Loves You Just the Way You Are, but he refuses to leave you that way. He wants you to be **Just** like **Jesus***.

Now I ask you: "Who wouldn't want to be just like Jesus?" Lucado believes that God can no more leave a life unchanged than a mother can leave a tear untouched. (He has a very nice way with words, don't you think?)

And he literally gets right to the heart of the matter. Beginning in chapter one, he offers his insightful thoughts on how to have a heart like Jesus – citing Scripture verses throughout for discussion and meditation.

From there he goes on, inviting his readers to consider how one's heart can become forgiving; compassionate; listening; God-intoxicated, worship-hungry, focused, honest; pure; hope-filled; and enduring.

Lucado asks the question; "What if, for one day and one night, Jesus lives your life with his heart? Your heart gets the day off, and your life is led with the heart of Christ – a heart that is peaceful, compassionate, loving, and spiritual." He believes that God's plan for us is nothing short of a new heart.

In John's fourteenth chapter (verse 11) Jesus says "I am in the Father and the Father is in me." And so it seems that Jesus wants to be in us. If you haven't already done so, why not invite him in and see what he has in mind?

After all, Jesus spent the last three years of his life giving his disciples a heart like his. Up to that point they had been pretty much ordinary people, just like us.

UNSUNG HEROES

Making a Difference was the headline and lead story in the *Burlington County Times* for the first several days of the New Year. At first, I thought, with all that's going on in our world these days – the economy, domestic violence, international affairs, global warming - "is making a difference" really deserving of front page coverage?

After a few moments thought, I decided the answer must be YES; particularly when you understand what the editor is trying to do – i.e., "recognize people in our community who work quietly behind the scenes, helping to make Burlington County a better place to live."

Featured are several "unsung heroes" who have given unselfishly of their time and talents and, yes, of their dollars also, to help others in need. A youth coordinator, a school custodian, and a lawyer, to mention a few! Ordinary people doing extraordinary things!

Now, does that sound familiar to any of you? Yes, I'm referring to you. As individuals and as a church body, you have been doing extraordinary things for people in need. And not just here in Burlington County, but throughout the world. For example:

Those of you who, through your weekly offering have been giving three (3) per cent of it to the ELCA World Hunger Appeal;

Those of you who gave Thanksgiving bags and baskets to neighbors not blessed as we are; Each of you Needle and Thread ladies who have invested your talents and countless hours preparing hundreds of blankets for the needy, both here and abroad;

Shawl Sharers who, last year, knitted/crocheted hundreds of shawls for shut-ins and persons across the country;

All of you who, through Rainbow of Hope's mentoring process, are helping homeless women become contributing citizens of our society;

Men's Prayer Breakfast members who have contributed hundreds of dollars over the years to Habitat for Humanity and other charities.

Oh, the list goes on and on thanks to all of you who have been gifted by God and are sharing with others. Yours is a Social ministry, a Stewardship ministry and, yes, an Evangelism ministry reaching out in love, expecting nothing in return.

Blessed to be a blessing *and* making a difference! How cool is that!

GOOD NEWS FROM CAMDEN

I *Love to Tell the Story of unseen things above, of Jesus and his Glory, of Jesus and his love....*

You remember the melody I'm sure, of one of my favorite hymns... How very thankful we should be for gifted musicians like Katherine Hankey and William E. Fisher who wrote the lyrics and the music of this lovely hymn.

And you know what? I love to tell a story, too, especially when it's a story about someone who was lost, but now is found.

Many of you remember a former Intern of ours some years back. Giselle Coutinho, now serves as pastor at Bridge of Peace Lutheran Church in Camden. This is a story she shared with her Lutheran pastor companions during a recent group study meeting.

It's a story of a woman who attended Bridge of Peace and took a seat in the rear of the church. Pastor C. noticed her and could see that she seemed to be quite upset about something; so she asked if she could help in some way. And then she listened.

Her guest stated that her mother had just died a few hours earlier that same morning. She declined Pastor C.'s offer of communion, stating that she had not gone to church for the past thirty-five years and did not feel worthy of Christ's grace and forgiveness. (Isn't this reminiscent of the young woman at Jacob's well who found Jesus, her Savior, also a good listener?)

It was obvious to pastor that the woman was repentant of her sins, and she encouraged the woman to reconsider her decision, even suggesting that the two of them commune together. Pastor explained our Lutheran understanding that the Sacraments are about Christ's forgiveness and not about our being good enough; and that they are a free gift of God's grace to all believers. In the end the two women shared communion together. Her last words before leaving: "I am so relieved and so grateful", and "I'll be back". And, sure enough, she has been back every week since.

But wait! There's more.

To be certain that I had all the facts straight, I phoned Pastor C. with a few questions. She returned my call on a following Sunday and, praise God, she added that a non- believer had just told one of her church members that she "wanted to turn her life over to Christ." Pastor C. and her congregation prayed over her and invited her to return the next day for their Vacation Bible School "kick off". They could use some help in the kitchen. She did return, and she brought two of her nieces with her. Good story, or what?!

I asked pastor if word of mouth was getting around about Bridge of Peace; and she replied that her church is much like the new churches we read and hear about in the Book of Acts, thanks to the likes of Paul and Peter and Jesus' disciples.

Stay tuned! Some pretty cool things are going on with our sisters and brothers at Bridge of Peace in Camden.

P.S. I forgot to mention: This story came to me compliments of Pastor Mangiante who also likes to tell a good story. Feel free to pass it forward.

MONICA'S PERSONAL STORY

A few years ago Pastor Jost received an email from Mark Hanson, our then Presiding Bishop of ELCA. The subject: Reflections on Evangelism. Among the many insights shared by the bishop was one in particular that caught my attention. He said "Personal stories are a powerful tool." I couldn't agree with him more.

Monica Dixon shared her personal story during one of our Wednesday morning Bible studies a few months back Before I get to that, let me tell you a little of what I know about her. She and her husband, Bill, are parents of three children, and normally attend our Sunday evening worship service. She is employed as a nurse at the Masonic Home in Burlington Township. Most recently she has been very involved with the settlement of our refugee family, assisting with hospitality, medical matters, transportation, and job placement. Here is her story, just as she gave it to me.

One day at work last December I had a conversation with my friend, Joel, about his wife, Brandy, who was not coping well since the loss of her mother. I told Joel about the difficulties that I was having coming to terms with my father's death even though fourteen months had passed. I shared with him the conversation I had with Pastor Stoner about my feeling of grief. Pastor explained to me that what I was feeling was quite normal. I explained to Joel that Brandy had to complete her grieving process. Otherwise, later it would come back. It just doesn't go away because we don't want to deal with it.

Then something really cool happened. I told my friend all about Jesus. This was the first time I ever talked about Jesus at work, and I have to say it really felt good to tell my friend about the love of Jesus.

We had a really deep conversation about life. I asked Joel, "Do you think all there is to life is to raise our families, pay our bills, then we die, and that's it?" Then I told him all about Jesus – how he came to live among men and to save the world. Jesus showed the world that everyone, rich or poor, slave or master is worthy to gain entrance to God's Kingdom. Joel told me that he didn't feel worthy because of some of the things he had done in the past. I said to Joel "Jesus came to earth for sinners like you and me. All you have to do is ask for his forgiveness and you will be forgiven.

This conversation took place before last Christmas. I bought Joel a Bible. This is probably the best Christmas present that I ever bought anyone. Since then I have been asking Joel almost every week to come with us to our Sunday night worship service, and I pray that he will come. One of these weeks he will, I'm sure, because I have faith that the Holy Spirit is working on him; and I'm not giving up.

Let's all pray with Monica, and for Joel and his wife, Brandy.

EVER ALERT

T hose of us here at St. Paul's, who have participated in the Adult Forum discussions held in the Music room between worship services, have had the opportunity to become acquainted with Gail Allgood. I really can't say I know her well, but let me tell you a little of what I do know.

Gail actively entered into our forum discussions. While some of us were more comfortable listening, Gail seemed quite at ease commenting on whatever it was we were talking about. This seemed especially so when our discussion centered upon the church, our faith, or upon Jesus Christ.

So it came as no surprise to me when she related a story to us of a conversation she had with a gentleman whom she met during a Crop Walk some years ago... It seemed this gentleman observed that Gail was walking with others from St. Paul's, and so he began to question her about our church.

Now Gail had remarked to some of us, on occasion, how welcoming she found St. Paul's to be. (She was relatively new to our congregation). So she didn't hesitate to share this information with her walking companion. And his interest grew.

Perhaps you can guess what followed. That's right! Before long, he was attending our Saturday night worship services and also taking part in Pastor Stoner's Wednesday night Bible study.

Ever alert, Gail recognized an opportunity to share her faith with a person who apparently had a desire to become better acquainted with our Lord Jesus, and she took advantage of that opportunity. Nice going, Gail!

Opportunities to witness our faith can arise any time and any place. Perhaps you have had an evangelical experience like this. Did it make you feel good? Did you want to share it with others?

WHAT WOULD JESUS DO?

This month I would like to ask you a question, and then I will close with a promise. First, the question!

Do you think there is any way that parents can learn from their children? For years I thought it very unlikely, perhaps impossible. But lately, I've been finding out from personal experience, that it's not only possible; but, in my case, it's become a matter of fact.

Every Father's Day many of us dads receive a large, colorful card from our children telling us how much they love us etc.; etc., etc. Well, this year my son John and his family not only sent me a card, but, a couple of days later John also sent me an e-mail which read: "Pop, I want to thank you for being an example of what a husband and father should be."

If he had said that to me face-to-face, I'm not sure how I would have responded. But, given a chance to think about it for a while, I said to him, "John, if truth be known, I've been learning from you for some time now.

Fast forward a couple of weeks.

We all had just come off the beach at Long Beach Island on one of those steamy, hot days a few weeks ago. As was our custom, we showered, ate dinner, and then headed up to the Skipper Dipper ice cream parlor for our dessert. I counted the number of flavors posted on the wall. There were twenty-six of them. My favorite is Hunka Junka PB Fudge on a waffle cone.

A couple of picnic tables were available on the patio outside, so we chose to finish our treats there. It wasn't but a few minutes, however, before our leisure was interrupted by the loud roar of a motorcycle approaching the corner light, just a few yards away.

To our dismay, the cyclist failed to bring his cycle to a complete stop, and he fell off, rather awkwardly.

Our son, John abandoned his ice cream and rushed to the man's side as he lay sprawled near the curb in obvious pain. Once certain the man could stand, John helped him to his feet, and offered to walk him home some two blocks away.

While all this was going on, I chose to finish my cone, wondering why anyone in his right mind would want to ride a motor cycle. It's just my opinion, of course, but isn't that something like an accident looking for a place to happen?

As we headed home, I began thinking more positively of what John had done. It occurred to me that his quick response to the man's need was, indeed, another act of kindness on his part. He had just helped someone, a neighbor, if you will, who clearly needed help. This seemed to me to be a story much like that of the Good Samaritan who helped the Jewish person who had been attacked by bandits while walking to Jericho, beaten up, and left half dead.

Being kind to others is something that seems to come easily to John – often enough that it prompted me to say to him once, "John, how is it you always seem to be on the alert for opportunities to help other people?" His response: "Dad, I pray every day God will give me opportunities."

Oh! My promise! I promise I will do my best to stop bragging so much about our offspring.

HERE'S THE PROOF

Whenever I serve as a Communion Assistant, if given a choice, I prefer serving the wine rather than the bread because, when handling the bread, I usually leave a trail of crumbs along the altar floor. And, so it was one Easter morning when I had a most unusual experience. As I proceeded along the communion rail, I came before a young woman whom I neither knew nor recognized. To my surprise, she looked up at me and confessed, "I am a sinner." Well, this had never happened to me before, and I was a little surprised. Not knowing quite what to say, I leaned toward her and said what first came to mind: "We are all sinners."

Afterward, it struck me that this was a rather lame response on my part. If I had been better prepared with the words on my lips, I could have added, "but now we are all saved." And I thought how neat it would have been if I had pointed to the chalice in my right hand, and said, "here's the proof." But, "clutz" that I am, I blew a grand opportunity to speak of God's truth.

Lesson: Always be prepared! We never know when God will give us a chance to witness to his love.

Some of you who have been attending the 11 a.m. worship service may have noticed a new face among our communion assistants. Her name is Amy Beacherer, and she serves every Sunday she can. I thought this quite commendable, so, one day I asked her why. She was quite forthright with her reply, so I found a pencil and began making notes.

Amy said that for most of her adult life, she has felt the Lord calling her to become a Eucharistic Minister, but she never had opportunity to be formerly trained to do this. She was pleasantly surprised, of course, when she learned of our need for Communion Assistants. And, with encouragement from Kathleen Johnson and Pastor Esposito to "do it", Amy has discovered a way to become an active member of our church family. She used the term "uplifting "to describe her worship experience since joining us at St. Paul's. Nice lady!

I should mention also that Amy is a licensed professional counselor and has her doctorate degree in clinical psychology. Her husband, Rudy, is also a doctor and works as an Emergency Room physician at a hospital in Warren, New Jersey.

When one singles out an individual and praises him or her, as I may have done here with Amy, I realize there are many more new members whose presence and participation in St. Paul's ministries are also well worth noting. Our thanks upon thanks to all of you who are sharing your gifts and talents in so many ways. Together we will make disciples for Jesus and grow His kingdom.

WE'VE GOT TO DO IT FOR THE KIDS

S ome time ago a friend and I visited a family whose Sunday worship attendance had become somewhat sporadic. Our purpose was simply to let them know that they were missed. We didn't want them to feel that their absence had gone unnoticed.

Their two children were watching television in the family room as we adults chatted in the kitchen. At one point my companion said something that has stayed with me ever since. He said, "We've got to do it for the kids." What he meant was it's really critical that we parents help our children develop the habit of regular Sunday school and church attendance.

And it's true, isn't it? Especially now, with drugs and guns, sex and violence, our kids have so much more to deal with than we had a generation ago. Hardly a day passes that we don't hear or read of another murder – or rape – or abuse of a child or spouse. And more and more, it's kids not yet in their teens who are perpetrating these crimes on other kids. We have to ask WHY!!

Some say the cause of this escalating violence can be traced directly to what our children are seeing on television. And, of course, they are right. Others say it's guns and the easy access to guns. And they are correct also, as are those who maintain that the need for two incomes in the family deprives many of our children of the love and attention they need and deserve.

All of this is true; but perhaps more than anything, we should be mindful of something else that is missing in the lives of many families. What could this be? Could it be that not enough of our families are finding their way to church on Sunday mornings? The bishop of our church synod recently cited an alarming statistic.

He reported that over fifty percent of our New Jersey population does not attend church. And yet, it's here in church and Sunday school where our children have a chance to learn how to live their lives – where they can learn about loving and forgiving, and caring and sharing. Oh sure, an hour in Sunday school may not rank number one on a youngster's list of favorite things to do; but, you know what? Years from now, those same kids are going to thank their parents for loving them enough to get them to Sunday school and church, where they were able to find a right direction for their lives.

It doesn't matter a whole lot what church or Sunday school they attend. I have heard Pastor Jost say any number of times "We're like Walmart - open every Sunday. And for those parents who work on Sunday, many churches, like ours, offer worship services on Saturday night. We need to remember that it's the kids who are not just our future, but our present, as well. And it's these kids about whom we should be most concerned.

BEING EVANGELICAL

At one of our recent Church Council meetings we were privileged to have in attendance our New Jersey Synod Bishop, Roy Riley. At one point during the meeting Bishop Riley paid St. Paul's a fine compliment, saying that ours is a grand congregation. To support this statement, he cited many of the global ministries in which we are active. Just to name a few: our splendid record of benevolence giving over the years, our worldwide missionary support, and our support of Christian Children both here and abroad.

Lest we become too full of ourselves, however, it's important that we acknowledge the Holy Spirit's involvement here. And there is much yet to be done. All one has to do is take notice of the empty pews around us on Sunday morning.

Bishop Riley pointed out that fifty per cent of New Jersey's population is unchurched. And we are told that many of these simply need to be invited. We need to reach out to them, invite them to come and see what St. Paul's is like, and make them feel welcome. And we have the potential to do it. The sign on our front lawn identifies us as St. Paul's Evangelical Lutheran Church. Let's not forget the evangelical part.

Most of us would probably agree that, morally, our nation is in a state of poor health. Every day we are bombarded by the media with news of crime, racial unrest, child abuse, and on and on. Yet we have to believe that our Lord has the power to change all this. But he needs our help.

How many times have we been told that we are the church and that each and every one of us are to be evangelical – simply by living lives that are Christian – and by being alert to opportunities that God gives us to reach out and speak to others of Jesus Christ and what he has cone for us.

Please accept my apology if all of this sounds so very pious. It very well may not be my place to say all this, but I really feel that, with prayer, we can be true disciples for Christ.

OH, TO BE YOUNG AGAIN

I've been saving this story for a year now. It's a true story -- an Easter story, which Jean Grimm told me about her four-year-old grandson named Hunter.

Like all of us, Hunter had heard the Easter story in Sunday School on Easter morning - all about what Jesus had done for us on the cross - and afterward. This story thrilled Hunter so much he couldn't wait to tell someone about it. So, when Hunter and his mom arrived at school the next day, there was no holding him back. The very first thing, Hunter asks his teacher, "Miss Christine, did you know that Jesus died on the cross to save us from our sins?"

Well! Both teacher and mother were quite taken by surprise at Hunter's proclamation. It obviously made quite an impression on Miss Christine - so much so that she commented on it to Lisa, Hunter's mother, several times since. I'd like to believe Hunter's great news may have freshened her faith a little, too. Who knows? Maybe she passed this story along to some of her teacher acquaintances, or perhaps to her own children. Who can know how far this lad's witness might have taken wing?

One has to wonder if Hunter's Sunday school teacher might have told her class to keep this story a secret, knowing full well how difficult it is for four-year-olds to keep a secret. Oh, to be young again, and free of the apprehensions we have as adults.

I wonder, too, if perhaps the Holy Spirit might have somehow planted Galatians 6:6 in Hunter's mind: "Those who are taught the word must share in all good things with their teacher."

Thank you, Jean, for this lovely story. And thank you, Lord, for all of our Sunday school teachers and for all of the four-year-olds like Hunter.

TWO BY TWO

S ome time ago, Pastor Jost opened his Chimes column (Pastor's Corner) with a statement Jesus makes in Revelation 21: "See, I am making all things new." I can't be certain, but Pastor may have been likening this to all the new activities going on at St. Paul's – such as a new concept in stewardship ... a new plan to hire a youth and family director ... build new buildings... explore new ways of doing ministry ... finding new ways of telling the old, old story.

With the arrival of spring, we are seeing new growth in many ways: trees sprouting forth new buds, the earth yielding new flowers, and here at St. Paul's we are planning new growth as well. Just as Jesus sent his disciples, two by two, into the world (Mark 6:7), so he will do with us.

Pastor Stoner and Pastor Johnson are making plans to send us out into our "world" to sow God's seed. We, too, will be God's messengers as we go, two by two, knocking on doors to invite our neighbors to join us for Easter worship. For some participants, this may be a new experience, but we will be going with Jesus' promise that we have nothing to fear. "Remember, I am with you always." (Mt. 28:20)

But we may still be wondering what we will say? How about something like this: "Happy Easter! If you don't have a church home, please come and worship with us. You would be most welcome at St. Paul's." That's it! Simple!

Some may ask, "How many homes will we visit?" Answer: Our goal is to send twelve pairs to ten homes. -- about one hour of our time.

Others, "When will this happen? Answer: The afternoon of the first Sunday before Palm Sunday.

And still others may wonder what's in it for us? How about an opportunity to help fulfill God's purpose for us – a chance to bear fruit – a time to sow God's seed – a chance to be what we claim to be: evangelical.

THE EASTER STORY - ONE WORTH TELLING

C hristians world-wide revere the story of Easter as much as any other in Scripture. It's a story not only worth telling, but telling well. With that in mind, I took my Strong's Concordance from the shelf to see exactly what the Bible had to say about Easter. To my complete surprise, I discovered that the term Easter is found only once in all of Scripture, that being in the King James Version – Acts 12:4. In my own church at St. Paul's, we use the New Revised Standard Version, where we find that Easter is replaced with Passover, a word that is thought by Biblical scholars to be more correct.

Next, I went to the Internet and googled "Easter." What did I find there? Very little I thought would be of interest to you. A lot of ambiguity like: the term Easter was derived from the Greek word PASKHA and the Hebrew PESAKH; and the Modern English version is speculated to have been developed from the Old English term EASTRE or EOSTRE. Oh, and the Continental Germanic peoples reconstructed the word as OASTRA. YAWN!!

About that time, I was thinking: Dave, let's cut to the chase. For goodness sake, go to the Bible. That's the best place to learn about Easter. Yes! I know that. But everybody already knows the Easter story. Why not just tell them how much you love the story. Tell it in your own words.

Imagine actually being there as Mary Magdalene and the other Mary arrive at the tomb. Can you picture what was going on? An earthquake, for heaven's sake! It must have been bedlam. And then, an angel of the Lord rolling back the stone! And the guards passing out!

Then the angel actually spoke to the women. "Don't be afraid. He isn't here! He is risen from the dead…. Come, see…." Can you picture the two women staring at each other in awe – then running to tell the disciples the good news? Imagine the bewilderment, the excitement, the wonder, the anxiety, and the JOY.

And, what must it have been like on the streets and in the market places? People running about shouting, "Did you hear the news about that man, Jesus, who was crucified last Friday? Some are saying he's alive! Others asking, "How can that be?" Another lady was heard to have said that Jesus actually met with his disciple friends on Sunday night, and that he even showed them the wounds in his hands and his side. Another man was telling a group by the well that he believes the story is true. "It might be a miracle," he said," but, I still believe it. Have you forgotten what he did at the wedding ceremony in Cana when he actually turned casks of water into wine?"

And another replying,"That's right! And I still remember when Jesus raised Lazarus from the dead; and he had been dead for almost a week. So, I have no problem believing God can raise up his own son."

His friend added, "my friend, Cleopas, told me that he and one of his friends actually met Jesus that same day, while they were heading for Emmaus. So, it's got to be true.

And, so it went, 0n and on,

Matthew tells the story so beautifully in his 28th chapter. And so do the other Gospel writers. It's a story worth reading and worth telling, again and again – because it's true.

A BAILOUT FOR THE NEEDY

C an we possibly find an upside to the economic collapse we experienced back in 2008-2009?

As we gathered for our first congregational meeting in February to consider the spending plan for the year ahead, Pastor Jost posed what I believed to be a very relevant question: How had we been blessed during the week just past?

Notwithstanding our stagnant economy, I believe that most of us have to admit to being blessed many times over by our Lord. When we acknowledge this to be true, how then, are we to respond to this benevolence of his? Trevor Shell got it right, I believe, when he pointed out at one of the meetings that the reason we are here is to glorify God. If we can accept this as true, how is it that we can discontinue support to so many of the benevolence ministries that we have supported in the past?

When the congregation decided to withdraw support to such ministries as the Bosnia International Service Team, Rainbow of Hope, and World Hunger, it seemed to me that we were taking a giant step backward. Aren't these the very people that Jesus served – the poor and the needy? How do we glorify God when we deny them our support?

I see this as not just a stewardship issue but an issue that impacts upon our outreach to the unchurched as well. We identify ourselves as St. Paul's Evangelical Lutheran Church. But I believe that we will never realize our potential as being evangelical stewards until we first realize we can live comfortably on ninety percent of what God has given us and returning ten percent to those who are in such dire need. I read recently that more than 800 million people in the world are undernourished.

I have always believed that, when we bear fruit for God and grow his church, the money will follow. When we fill our pews with disciples who love God and respond in kind to his benevolence, he will entrust to us even more. Unfortunately, for this to happen, it may be that 80 per cent of the solution will have to come from the 20 per cent of our already committed members. It just may be that it is this smaller group that best understands that everything – EVERYTHING – we have has been entrusted to us by our loving Lord.

hanks be to God, there is still time to turn this around. Some have already responded and are digging deeper; and plans are being made to convene the congregation again in mid-year to determine how much of the shortfall has been closed.

Meanwhile, perhaps it's time for all of us to ask ourselves some serious questions, - like: Are there others whose needs are greater than ours?

Do we really need to spend so much for Christmas presents this year?

Do we really need that new 52 inch TV with surround sound and a hundred umpteen channels that we'll never watch?

You know, we've heard a lot about bailouts in recent years. Bailouts for the banks; bailouts for the auto workers! What about a bailout for the needy?

On a lighter note! Maybe it would be nice if we could all heed the advice Jiminy Cricket gave his good friend, Pinnochio: "Let your conscience be your guide."

A HOME RUN OPPORTUNITY

H appy Easter, everyone! How blessed we are to have been able to join in the celebration of arguably the most wonderful event of all time, the Resurrection of our Lord and Savior, Jesus Christ. And with this resurrection comes the awesome guarantee that, as believing children of our Father in heaven, we have the promise of eternal life with Him in his heavenly home.

You may think it irreverent of me, but with all due respect, I would like to call to mind another great event we celebrate every year about this time – the opening of yet another baseball season.

How sweet it is: the crack of the bat and the roar of the crowd! Oh, I know! It's not an act of God, and it's not something we can expect to enjoy forever in heaven. At least, I don't recall any mention of it in Scripture. But think about it: another twenty-six weeks of baseball before the season ends.

The article that appears below was sent to me by my good friend, Don Rousseau, a member of Faith Lutheran Church in North Palm Beach, Florida, where our daughter, Linda, and her family also worship. Don writes an Outreach Challenge article for the Flame, which is Faith's monthly newsletter. His title for this article: IT'S A HOME RUN.

*   *   *

A home run by your favorite team is one of the greatest events in a baseball game, and a grand slam is even better. But there is another event that is significantly greater. It is seeing someone respond to the Gospel message and receive Jesus Christ as his Savior. As Christians, what greater excitement is there than seeing someone give his/her life to Jesus? Such an event is a miracle and greater than any home run. Also, salvation is an eternal event. And it is even more wonderful if that person, who has been saved, is someone with whom you have shared the Gospel.

In a survey, George Barna found that, in the U.S., one out of every three adults is classified as unchurched – meaning not having attended a church service of any type in the last six months. Statistically speaking then, of the next thirty persons you see, ten of them are unchurched.

What an opportunity for you and me.

LOVE

THE SPECTRUM OF LOVE

B illy Graham, Billy Sunday, Dwight Moody, and Corrie ten Boom are but a few of the distinguished evangelists I have written about over the years -- all of them staunch Christians, to be sure. To this august group we might add the name of David Livingstone, the beloved medical missionary who believed that, by combining healing with the Gospel, one would be living as Christ himself – just as Paul himself urges in his letter to the Ephesians. Eph.5:2.

But, what is it, do you suppose, that makes these people so extraordinary?

In his book, *The Greatest Thing in the World,* Henry Drummond described Livingstone as a missionary of love. The black men and women whom he served in Africa could not understand him, but they felt the love in his heart. Isn't this the very quality that anyone would need in order to become a devoted disciple of Jesus? Love!

While meeting with a small group of Christians one evening, Mr. Drummond was asked to read from Scriptures; so, he opened a small Testament and read from the 13th chapter of 1 Corinthians, a verse that many of you will recognize immediately. "And now abideth faith, hope, love, these three; but the greatest of these is love ...."

Then, setting aside his Bible, the author spoke at length of his thoughts about love. He first contrasts it with faith and charity and other virtues. Then he analyses it and, finally defends it as the greatest of all things.

But it was Drummond's analysis of love that, to me, was most

277

beautiful. He describes love as a compound thing -- like a beam of light that a man of science might pass through a crystal prism and see it come out the other side broken into its component colors – red, and blue, and yellow, violet, and orange and all the colors of the rainbow. So it is with Paul, he maintains, who passes this thing, love, through the magnificent prism of his inspired intellect, and then observes it broken down into its elements, what one might call the Spectrum of Love. Nine virtues which can be practiced every day and in every place of life: patience, kindness, generosity, humility, courtesy, unselfishness, good temper, guilelessness, and sincerity. I suggest that we could add a few of our own, such as friendliness, compassion, forgiveness; but Drummond chose just those nine which he goes on to examine in depth throughout his book.

He concluded his analysis by urging us to "have these things fitted into our characters." "That" he declared, "is the supreme work to which we need to address ourselves ….to learn Love."

LOVE AND EVANGELISM – GOOD COMPANIONS

A rtfully Yours is a charming gift shop on Main Street in Moorestown, New Jersey. As Laura and I drove by recently, we enjoyed reminiscing about some of the items we had purchased at this store over the years – several framed pictures and a flower center piece, to mention a few. As we continued home, it occurred to me that this might make for an interesting introduction to this month's article.

If you were an artist, and someone commissioned you to paint a picture that expressed love *artfully,* what would your picture look like when finished? Perhaps it might be something like the cover of our church bulletin a few weeks ago. You may recall it depicted what appeared to me to be a woman reading a Bible story to a young child sitting on her lap. Or it might be an illustration, something like Norman Rockwell's portrayal of a family about to enjoy a Thanksgiving Day meal. Another of my favorites is Warner Sallman's representation of *Christ at Hearts Door*, which shows Jesus knocking on the door to our heart, hoping to gain admittance because He loves us so. Until someone pointed it out to me, I never noticed that the door has no outside doorknob and can only be opened from within.

While thinking about how I might introduce this article, I asked myself that same question …how to portray love artfully; and I recalled recently seeing an elderly couple walking slowly toward me hand-in-hand, or it may have been arm-in-arm. And I thought to myself: what a delightful picture they made.

Maybe I'm getting sentimental in my old age, but seeing two people like that is pretty much how I perceive love and evangelism – as companions, each one a part of the other. When you think about it, you really can't be very good at one without being good at the other, can you?

You may recall my mention last month of Dr. Leo Bustaglia and his book *Born for Loving – Reflections on Loving.* Many of his reflections are quite good and, I believe, worthy of being shared. So, that's what I would like to do. Here are just a few:

* A day without having completed an act of love is a day lost.
* Every day I live I am more convinced that the waste of life lies in the love we have not given.
* The most essential quality for a lasting relationship is the ability to communicate.
* Praise, like love, is only meaningful when freely-shared.
* ....sound counsel: "Do unto others what you would have them do unto you."
* Listening is an act of love … it's a learned art.
* A simple hug is one of the most convenient and inexpensive therapies available.
* Giving *in* is an important kind of giving when people love each other.
* Love words that count: "Thank you"" – "I love you" – "I'm sorry" – "What can I do for you" –
* "Good for you" – "Well done" – "I'm proud of you." Bustaglia also draws on the thoughts of other notables.
* You learn to love by loving – Aldous Huxley
* Loneliness and the feeling of being unwanted is the most terrible poverty – Mother Theresa When I finished Dr. Bustaglia's book, I felt the need to ask God to help me do better at loving. May I suggest that this might be a kind of prayer we all might ask of Him?

UNCONDITIONAL LOVE

D aisy is a rescue dog adopted a couple of years ago by our daughter, Linda, and her husband, Bert. Daisy's story of being lost and then found has a sad, almost heart-rending beginning that gives way to an ending that I believe you will find most delightful.

Daisy had been abandoned by a family whose home had been foreclosed. How long she had been alone on the streets is not known; but, by the time she was found and taken to a shelter, she was very thin, and her body was covered with fleas. She was quickly transferred to the Everglades Retriever Rescue Shelter where she was examined and treated by a vet.

Meanwhile, Linda had registered with the shelter, hoping to find a replacement for their golden retriever, Zoey, who had died recently. After completing a six-page questionnaire, Linda and her family were found to be a satisfactory fit for Daisy; and the adoption was consummated.

The attached photo of Daisy and Bert was taken recently at the dog's estimated age of two to three years. When we received the photo, I immediately was struck by what appeared to me to be the kind of unconditional love that Daisy and Bert seemed to be feeling for each other. I could almost imagine Bert saying to her "You were lost, but we found you. We chose you; and now we have come to love you. And we will never let you go, no matter what."

And, in return, is it too much of a stretch to imagine Daisy's reply to her master: "Thank you so much for choosing me. I love you back and I will do anything you ask and go anywhere you send me.

Perhaps I'm reading too much sentiment into this photo. But isn't this the kind of unconditional love that God bestows on us – the kind of love that keeps giving and giving?

Where might our Master want us to go? And what might He want us to do.? You know as well as I that Christ's Great Commission found In Matthew 28: 19-20 tells us where to go; that is, into the world; and what to do; that is, make disciples and teach them to obey all of His commands. And He promises to be with us always.

I believe God will help us with this because, after all, it is in keeping with his will and purpose for us.

LOVE 101

When our Youth Advisor once asked if I would lead a one-week, small group Bible study, I accepted – reluctantly. By the end of that week, my mindset had undergone a complete change. Why?

To begin with, she explained I was not to actually *teach* the course. I was simply to serve as a *facilitator*. And what a relief it was to find that my dictionary defined this term as "to make something easy.... less difficult."

Our assignment was to examine how, as Christians, we learn to share, give, grow, love, and praise – one virtue for each day of the week. Our study guide contained several beautiful Bible stories featuring such notables as Ruth, Elisha, and Paul, and how these five virtues were brought to light by the way they lived.

Thursday morning was my favorite. *How we love* was the day's topic. Jesus has quite a bit to say about love in the Gospels and, of course, so does Paul in his epistles.

As an additional source, I went to Henry Drummond's classic, *The Greatest thing in the* World, in which he so beautifully describes how Paul passes this supreme quality, love, through the magnificent prism of his inspired intellect, and observes as it comes out on the other side broken into nine elements: patience, kindness, generosity, humility, courtesy, unselfishness, good temper, guilelessness, and sincerity.

So I wrote these ingredients on the board and asked the group how else, in their opinion, love might be defined. By the time we finished, our board looked like this: Love is obedient, helpful, friendly, giving, inviting, joyful, forgiving, encouraging, fruitful, caring, honest, sacrificing, active, fearless, listening and disciplining(both found several times in Proverbs), also humble, transforming, joined to Christ. No doubt, you could probably add a few more. How about: Love is being gracious, serving, neighborly, and glorifying God.

Wow! Just imagine what our world would be like if everyone tried to build some of these virtues into their character. Food for thought! Please, stay with me on this.

Is it possible that our children could be taught to love? Oh, I know that it happens for the few who attend Sunday schools and, I suppose some of our parochial schools do a pretty good job of it; but, what about the millions of our children attending public schools?

Think about it: a course that could be taught to all children regardless of their race, or their religion, or their cultural background – a course that would invite kids to delve into what it's really like to be a loving person.

I believe our educators could develop such a course. After all, they're already being taught at an early age that a sentence is comprised of three elements - a subject, a verb, and a predicate. In their science classes, they are learning about the Periodic Table of Elements – manganese, zinc, titanium, and many others. Why not also teach about the elements of love? It could be added to their school curriculum and taught, just like math, and science, and the languages. A few chapters might even be devoted to such renowned personages as Albert Schweitzer, Mahatma Gandhi, Martin Luther King, Mother Theresa – all people known for having lived lives of love and tolerance. Who knows? Maybe there would be less violence in our schools and neighborhoods. Perhaps people of different cultures might become more tolerant of one another

Bottom line! If love is not being taught in our public schools, it should be.

You may have noticed that no mention was made about being -- evangelical. Let's think about that for a moment.

We have been taught that God is Love, and that he wants us to love one another. Who knows? Maybe if we teach our youngsters how to love, they might go home and help their parents do the same.

LOVE IN ACTION

Can anything good come out of the flood that recently devastated so many of our friends and neighbors? I believe it not only can, but it already has. All one had to do was witness the overflow of love in action demonstrated by the hundreds of volunteers who gave of their time and energy to relieve the suffering – carrying any number of ruined possessions out to the curb for pick-up – providing food for a meal and a temporary home – donating not just money, but pots and pans, lawn mowers and tools – hauling buckets of mud from inundated basements – consoling with hugs and prayers. And this doesn't even begin to scratch the surface.

Matthew Henry reminds us that "True Christians will feel for their brethren under afflictions" and adds "If all mankind were true Christians, how cheerfully would they help one another ..."

We have heard many times over the years God's Great Commandment to love Him with all our heart, soul, mind, and strength, and that we are to love our neighbor, as well. Pastor recently invited us to imagine how beautiful our world would be if we loved our neighbors as God wants us to. One of the beautiful hymns we sing says it so well:

> *"Jesu, Jesu, fill us with your love, Show us how to serve the neighbors We have from you ..."*

Pastor harked back to the Marshall Plan. (I believe this was during President Truman's administration) – a plan that helped our neighbors (and former enemies in Germany) recover from the ravages of WWII.

We have seen such a "plan" at work in our neighboring communities, haven't we?

Perhaps God has used this dreadful flood to bring out the best in people – love and kindness, caring and sharing - qualities of true Christians – followers of Christ.

What does all of this have to do with evangelism? I'm glad you asked.

First, one of the ways we witness our faith is by the way we live. Isn't that so? But, to respond to this further, I have to look to my son, John, and his wife, Laura.

Their home also has been damaged by rising flood waters. Thank God, they have been blessed with loving neighbors who came to their aid without even being asked.

But, you know what! John and Laura gave back a lot, too. The prayed; and they also acted on their prayers.

When he learned that the home of one of his neighbors had been condemned after flood damage, John contacted a nearby home builder who leveled the damaged home and replaced it with a lovely new home – at no cost.

Notwithstanding how much aid these flood victims received from insurance and FEMA and donations, it's really hard, I believe, for us to comprehend what these people went through. But John and Laura knew firsthand how desperate their needs were – and still are.

Oh yes! To conclude this story on a happy note, I am pleased to report the neighbors whom they helped have now asked John and Laura if they could go to church with them after they get settled in.

GOD'S IMMENSE LOVE

Would you agree that someone who chooses to write should be well-grounded in the subject about which he/she is writing? Of course you would. A biographer, for example, has no business writing about someone without having first researched his subject thoroughly.

Neither would a Time magazine reporter be assigned to recount Middle East activities without having first been in that region for some time.

Doesn't it follow that someone who chooses to write about something like evangelism should be experienced in that field – like maybe an evangelist, or at least someone who knows Jesus Christ intimately and is prepared to tell others about Him. But, when I went to my dictionary to see how the word evangelist is defined, I found five definitions: (1) a preacher of the Gospel; (2) any of the writers of the four gospels; (3) a revivalist; (4) an occasional or itinerant preacher; and (5) a person marked by a zealous enthusiasm for any cause.

Clearly, this is an exercise I should have undertaken years ago, before beginning to write these evangelism articles. Obviously, I am not a preacher. Neither am I an apostle, or a revivalist, or a zealot. What I am, I believe, is simply someone trying to help others understand that the reason why we are here is, first and foremost, to continue the work begun by Jesus and his disciples; i.e., to proclaim the good news of Jesus as best we can. At times I have tried to do this by highlighting the lives of notable Christians such as Albert Schweitzer, Dwight Moody, Corrie ten Boom, Peter Marshall, and others. There have been times also when I have tried to encourage readers to attend church and Bible Study regularly. After all, how can we speak to others about Jesus if we don't know him well ourselves?

But there have been times, I'm sure, when the point I was trying to make was unclear to you, or the article may have been totally unrelated to evangelism, or both.

So as to avoid this in the future, I plan to include in each article a passage from Scripture that clearly is evangelical – something that God says is good news for us and can be passed forward to others. All of us have favorite Bible stories. Think for a moment about some of your good news favorites while I tell you of one of mine.

It was a Saturday morning some years ago when I cautiously entered the sanctuary to borrow a hymnal from one of the back pews. I say "cautiously" because Pastor Jost was meeting with a youth group up front, and I didn't want to disturb them. All to no avail, however, as Pastor took notice of my entrance and declared to the group "Aha, here we have the pleasure of Mr. Pagenkopf's august presence; and I am sure that he can recite for you what is found in John, chapter three, verse sixteen. Go right ahead, Mr. P. we are all ears."

As you can imagine, I was struck dumb; and there was a rather prolonged silence before I realized that John 3:16 was one of my favorites (and one of yours too, I'm sure.) Hesitating for a moment, I began: "For God so loved the world that he gave his only Son, so that everyone who believes in him may not perish but have everlasting life." Thinking it more than likely that my pastor wouldn't give a second thought to asking for yet another recitation, I quickly grabbed a hymnal and high-tailed it out of the sanctuary.

Why is John 3:16 one of my favorite good news passages? Well, first of all, it's a familiar passage to many of us, or at least one that can be easily memorized. And it speaks of God's immense love for us. Can you imagine a God who loves us so much that he was willing to give away His only Son to die for us? And it's a true story, and one that promises eternal life to all believers. Not only is this Good News, but, in its telling, it is something by which we can fulfill His purpose for us to make disciples and grow his kingdom.

HUGS

I love them – especially when they come with a smile.

Is there anything more uplifting than a good squeeze and a pat on the back? Not that I'm aware of. And while you're at it, a tender "I love you" wouldn't hurt either. Sometimes, a handshake just isn't enough.

It's taken me a lifetime to appreciate how special a hug can be. I can remember when, as a young man arriving home from college or on leave from military service, greeting my dad with a firm handshake and a "how have you been?"- and mom with an affectionate kiss on the cheek and telling her how much I've missed her. But seldom, if ever, did I give a thought to how much they may have missed me, prayed for me, or loved me. Such thoughts just never crossed my mind.

But as we grow older and more mature, we learn to express our love for others more tenderly. As a husband and father, I have learned from every member of my family how heartwarming a simple hug can be.

And, how wonderful it is to greet members of our church family with smiles and well-wishes as we gather for worship, and as we *pass the peace* to one another during worship! Some have said they consider the *passing of the peace* one of the most meaningful parts of our worship service. I will stop short of suggesting a hug would be appropriate at that time. That I would leave to the discretion of our pastor. Indeed, it might justly be thought of as inappropriate, even awkward.

But let's all of us accept a good hug as a most wonderful expression of love.

When we love, we become more obedient to Jesus and his Great Commandment to love and make disciples. In truth, I believe we become more like him.

LOVE 1A

I f you read my previous article, you may recall that I tried to make a case that would require a course on love be taught to all public school students. Having thought about it since, I am more convinced than ever that such a course should be required study for all youth. Well, can you imagine my surprise when I discovered such a course has already been taught, albeit at the college level?

While browsing through several tables of books at a recent library used book sale – Laura and I seldom miss one – I discovered a book titled *Born for Love-Reflections on Loving* written by Leo Buscaglia. Some of you may have heard of him or perhaps even read him. At one time, five of his books appeared on the *New York Times Best Sellers* list.

It was back in the turbulent 1960s that Buscaglia's passion for love first attracted public notice. He was teaching a course for Special Education students at the University of Southern California, and, tragically, it was then that one of his students committed suicide. She was one of his brighter students and, as you might imagine, Buscaglia was devastated, so much so that, upon recovering, he felt moved to create a non-credit class, which he titled simply *Love 1A*. The class was so well-received that he prepared a manuscript loosely based on the thoughts he shared with his students. He found a publisher and was surprised to learn that no other author owned a copyright for a book titled *Love*. So, this became the title for his book. His message and delivery were so compelling that he was soon speaking at educational conferences nationwide.

David Pagenkopf

By the 1980s, he was often seen on national television, and he became the largest single money producer for PBS. Reaction to his dynamic, evangelical delivery on the topics of love and human relationships was unlike anything ever seen in educational circles. And it all began with his lecture notes for a class called *Love 1A*.

Dr. Buscaglia believes people need to accept that love is a positive choice everyone must make. And he adds that love needs to be evoked, studied, taught and practiced. To this I would add that teaching about love should begin early in a child's elementary school education.

WHAT DID YOU LEARN IN SCHOOL TODAY?

I t's been almost 150 years since Abraham Lincoln was assassinated. Three more incumbent presidents have been shot and killed since then – James Garfield, William McKinley, and John Kennedy. And, several others have survived attempts on their lives. – Theodore Roosevelt and his distant cousin, Franklin, Harry Truman, Gerald Ford, and Ronald Reagan.

Missing among those listed, of course, are scores of others around the world whose lives have been cut short by would-be assassins. One might dare say there has been an "open season" of sorts on world leaders and dignitaries. Some of you may be asking yourselves, "What is David getting at?" Just this!

We are living in a violent world, and neither anything nor anyone has been able to put a stop to it. Oh, I know! There have been any number of laws that have been enacted by our legislators – the Gun Control Act of 1968 following the murders of Martin Luther King and Robert Kennedy, the Brady Handgun Violence Prevention Act passed in 1993, the Violent Crime Control and Law Enforcement Act of 1994, to mention a few. Add to these, several gun "Bye- Back" laws that have been enacted in some states. But who can say to what extent these laws have suppressed violence in our country? People are still being killed by other people – Littleton, Colorado, Springfield, Oregon, Aurora, Colorado, Washington, D.C., Newtown, Connecticut, and Santa Barbara, California. On and on, it goes.

More recently, we hear reports of teenagers beating up helpless senior citizens, school children being stabbed by a demented youth. And now, the latest craze – Bullying!

It would be remiss of me, I believe, to raise this issue without offering some kind of solution. With my most recent article, you may recall I proposed love as the cure for violence, and that we begin teaching love in our public schools. To those of you who might view this as somewhat off the wall, or even hair-brained, I would say, "Nothing else seems to be working. Let's give it a try." I will concede that it's going to take a lot of time; but that's even more reason to get started now. With prayer, patience, and persistence, I believe love can change things for the better, especially when our efforts have Jesus' blessing.

Let's begin with teaching our children. Let's teach them how to be kind, caring, friendly, patient, forgiving, encouraging – all the elements of love.

Who knows? Maybe our children could teach their parents how to love. It doesn't seem to be working very well the other way around. Wouldn't it be something if daddy came home from work, took his seat at the dinner table, and asked his children the question all daddies like to ask, "Well, what did you learn in school today?", and then heard in reply, "Daddy, we learned all about love today." What an incredible dinner conversation that could turn out to be!

Please stay with me on this. I have a few more thoughts on the subject.

Who would be best-suited to teach about this love? Why, our teachers, of course. Here's another thought. How about offering the job to some of our retired teachers? A lot of our children have a warm spot in their hearts for the grandma and grandpa types. They have worlds of experience and know all about lesson plans and worksheets. Or they can go to Google and find over 400,000 lesson plans for every age and subject imaginable – lesson plans for K-12, for reading, science, language, social studies, and fractions. You name it.

The children could be given homework assignments related to the elements of love. Love clubs could be organized, just as they are for other school activities. What about text books? Well, I would recommend Leo Buscaglia's *Living, Loving, and Learning*, and his *Born for Love – Reflections on Loving*, or perhaps *Acts of Kindness – How to Create a Kindness Revolution* by Meladee and Hanoch McCarty.

Maybe the next step would be to turn this over to our Boards of Education. Wouldn't this fall into their bailiwick?

A CURE FOR VIOLENCE

I f you haven't noticed, there have been a flood of media reports about gun violence in America. These news accounts have become so constant that I have become numbed, almost indifferent, to them. There seems to be no remedy for this violence. The police don't seem to be able to stem the tide; and, for whatever reason, neither do our law makers. But, I have good news. In fact, I have a cure.

How about if we all learned how to love? It will take a long time to set things right, but, let's get started – now. And, let's begin with our children.

I know, you're probably thinking this guy is really "off the wall…. Get real! We're living in a world of reality now." And that would be true. All one has to do is read a newspaper or listen to the evening news. The reality is that we are living in a world of drugs, crime, hate, vice, terrorism, and guns. One might say it's always been that way. And, that may be true. But, does it have to go on forever? I don't think so. We have to stop doing nothing, and start doing what's right. "What would that be?" you might ask.

We've got to begin by consciously adopting into our characters those virtues that define l o v e. How about being friendly, kind, caring, patient, forgiving, encouraging, and discipline (as in tough love)? No doubt, you could add even more. Imagine what our world would be like if all people tried to do this.

Is it possible that our children could be taught how to love? Oh, I know it happens for the few who attend Sunday schools; and I suppose some of our parochial schools do a pretty good job of it. What about the millions of children attending public schools? A course that could be taught to all children regardless of race or cultural background – a course that would invite kids to delve into what it's really like to be a loving person.

I believe educators could devise such a course. If I'm not mistaken, our children are already being taught at an early age that a sentence is composed of three elements: a subject, verb, and predicate. In their science classes, they are studying the Periodic Table of Elements. Why not also teach them about the elements of love? Given some careful thought, I would hope our school boards of education would think favorably of adding such a course to their curriculums. Who knows, perhaps there might be less violence in our schools and neighborhoods, Maybe people of different cultures would become more tolerant of one another.

The bottom line! If love is not being taught in our schools, it should be. And, the same could be said of our homes, as well.

To any of you who may be wondering what love has to do with evangelizing, let me say this: If we love one another as Jesus teaches, wouldn't it be our next step to tell these people we love all about Jesus? A very strong bond exists, I believe, between loving and evangelizing.

UNDERSTANDING GOD'S LOVE

This month I would like to share with you two beautifully written verses depicting the vastness of God's love for us. This first verse is from the hymn, *The Love of God*, which I found in my devotional booklet. It goes like this:

> *Could we with ink the ocean*
> *Fill and were the skies*
> *Of parchment made,*
> *Where every stalk on earth a quill*
> *And every man a scribe by trade, to write the love of*
> *God above would drain the Ocean dry*
> *Nor could the scroll contain the whole*
> *Though stretched from sky to sky.*

The second verse is found in Paul's letter to the Ephesians (v. 18-19:): "And may you have the power to understand, as all God's people should, how wide, how long, how high and how deep his love is ... though it is too great to understand fully ..."

As we approach the end of the Lenten season, it seems to me that we might understand better this vastness of God's love when we reflect upon the gift of his Son whom he sent to die on the cross for our sins.

We all know, of course, the story of the crucifixion. But do we understand fully what Jesus really endured for us on that Good Friday so many years ago; - the mocking and the scourging at the hands of Caiaphas and the Roman soldiers; the physical beating inflicted; the whipping that cut into the skin and tissues of Jesus' shoulders and back; the crown of thorns pressed into his scalp; the gouging of the rough wood into his lacerated skin; the indescribable pain of heavy, wrought-iron nails being driven deep into the wood through his hands and feet; the searing agony as the cross is dropped into the hole prepared for it.

Not pleasant reading; that's for sure. But somehow, I believe that a greater appreciation and understanding of God's infinite love can be had as we ponder upon Jesus' appalling suffering and death.

Now we can look forward to the joyful good news of Easter morning as we celebrate Jesus' victory over death for us and his promise of eternal life with him in heaven. You can invite neighbors and friends to come with you to hear the Easter story. Many of them are waiting for an invitation – from you – to hear the wideness, the height, the length and the depth of God's love for them.

Printed in the United States
By Bookmasters